...lity Management

...ncepts, Techniques and Systems

Quality Management

Concepts, Techniques and Systems

Bholanath Das

Formerly, Senior Development Officer,
Department of Industrial Policy and Promotion,
Ministry of Commerce and Industry, Government of India,
New Delhi

New Century Publications
New Delhi, India

NEW CENTURY PUBLICATIONS
4800/24, Bharat Ram Road,
Ansari Road, Daryaganj,
New Delhi – 110 002 (India)

Tel.: 011-2324 7798, 6539 6605
Fax: 011-4101 7798
E-mail: indiatax@vsnl.com • info@newcenturypublications.com
www.newcenturypublications.com

Editorial office:
LG–7, Aakarshan Bhawan,
4754-57/23, Ansari Road, Daryaganj,

New Delhi – 110 022
Tel.: 011-4358 7398

First Published: **2013**

ISBN: **978-81-7708-341-5**

Published by New Century Publications and printed at Salasar Imaging Systems, New Delhi.

Designs: Patch Creative Unit, New Delhi.

PRINTED IN INDIA

for

parents, *Smt. Durga and Shri Fakir Charan Das*

with obeisance

and

life-partner, *Saraswati* with love

About the Book

Quality of products/services assumes great importance for manufacturers/providers in the modern competitive world. In fact, the quest for quality is essentially a search for competitiveness.

Quality being so critical to products and services, it is worth understanding what it is in its entirety—its evolution and definition; why it is so important for business and industry; and how to attain, maintain and manage quality of goods manufactured and services offered? This book attempts to provide comprehensive insights into all these aspects.

The target audience for the book includes practicing managers responsible for decision-making in an organization, professionals engaged in developing quality culture, and the academics including students who are training or being trained for quality management. These groups are directly or indirectly responsible to transform management philosophy, and create new visions for enterprises to integrate individual aspirations with organization's excellence.

Author's Profile

Bholanath Das retired as Senior Development Officer, Department of Industrial Policy and Promotion, Ministry of Commerce and Industry, Government of India, New Delhi. His distinguished career spanned over four decades and saw him in various senior positions in teaching, administration and policy formulation in India and abroad. Among other roles, he was the Joint Development Commissioner and Development Commissioner in-charge of Falta Special Economic Zone, Kolkata and Technical Advisor, Indian Investment Centre, Frankfurt, Germany. He also served as part of the faculty at IIT-Banaras Hindu University (BHU), Varanasi and National Institute of Technology, Rourkela. He holds the honour of being the first Indian Engineering Service (IES) professional from Odisha.

After retiring from active service, he is currently a consultant and an author. The opportunity to travel extensively across the globe sharpened his acumen for keen observation and broadened his perspective and horizon. His yearning for erudition and avid interest in writing and reading, places him as literati far above the ordinary. His debut book *Reflection* (2009) was well received amongst the masses. His literary work also includes publication of numerous articles in reputed journals and magazines across diverse topics.

He enjoys a unique distinction of academic excellence as the top ranker from the School Board (Orissa), Science Course (Utkal University) to Engineering (IIT-BHU) and Master of Business Management (FMS, Delhi University). He honed his specialization in quality management from Stockholm, Sweden.

Contents

Preface

In order to meet the challenges of today's dynamic market environment and to sustain and grow in the future, the need for establishing a quality organization and quality culture is obvious. Implementing quality management system in a business enterprise is one of the proven paths, for quality uniquely combines 'doing things right' and 'doing right things' in addition to integrating the process and the people for achieving desired product quality.

An honest attempt has been made to present a comprehensive guide on quality management with valuable insights into the concepts, tools, techniques and systems which contribute to improve quality. These have been developed, practiced and fine-tuned with carefully planned experimentation and direct shop floor experience.

The book cogently presents an overview of the evolution and development of the quality concept from the philosopher's view point to an integrated system of managing quality in industry. It carefully elaborates steps to be taken for implementing total quality systems approach for establishing quality culture in the business organization, combining theoretical aspects with practical experiences, emphasizing the need for application of tools and techniques for achieving continuous improvement of product quality in order to meet and exceed the customer's expectation.

The text is organized into 8 chapters, each chapter devoted to a specific aspect that forms part of the core content of the book. An outline of each chapter is as follows.

Chapter 1 introduces the subject 'quality', describes its importance in industry and explains how it is a novel approach to doing business for success. This chapter also contains a chapter-wise brief for readers' perusal.

Chapter 2 traces the concept of quality from pre-industrial era where the skilled craftsman maintained quality as a matter of his personal aggrandizement to the present day management of quality, 'total quality' in industry. It chronicles the contribution of pioneers and thinkers in the field of quality, such as Walter A. Shewhart, Edward Deming, Juran, Philip Crosby, and Feigenbaum among others and highlights the milestones in quality development.

Chapter 3 contains definition of quality, international and national quality standards and quality certification under ISO 9001. A synthesis of various definitions adopted by distinguished quality experts, quality association and the ISO is presented along with relevant standards and those adapted in India by Bureau of Indian Standards.

The procedure to be adopted by a business organization applying for certification under ISO 9001 along with benefits and responsibilities are comprehensibly explained for the benefits of the industry and consultants.

Chapter 4 provides an exhaustive description of the tools and techniques usually deployed for quality management in industry at present by quality consultants and practicing managers. The tools include the seven basic tools in addition to some recent developments and the fifteen techniques encompassing a wide range from general to specific application—SQC, Benchmarking, Kaizen, QFD, Six Sigma and the like. Care has been taken to specify advantages and limitations of the approaches for application.

Chapter 5 elaborates the development of quality control system from inspection of manufactured goods to total quality management through quality assurance, company wide quality, total quality and how the approaches applied systematically would result in establishing quality organization and quality culture.

Implementation of total quality systems in a company that has so far been following traditional methods for transiting to a quality organization is discussed in Chapter 6. The process being complex, simplified phase-wise guidelines with steps involved in each are presented along with concerns that need to be taken care of. It explains that the commitment of the senior management to involvement and participation of all employees for implementing quality improvement programme are important towards realizing the organizational goal.

Chapter 7 is a synthesis of theoretical aspects and results of on the job experience in quality consulting over a long period. It provides a well defined approach for the implementation of quality improvement programme in a going concern for its existing activity or launching a new product. The prerequisite and cautions are candidly explained for the benefit of practicing managers.

Chapter 8 sums up the essential elements for implementation of total quality as an optimal approach for achieving the organizational goal. Some practical tips are also provided for Indian companies: how they should proceed with managing change.

A case study on the implementing quality improvement project in a service organization, recently undertaken is also presented. The 'quality in practice' confirms the effectiveness of a pragmatic approach: management commitment for continuous improvement, empowerment of employees for involvement and application of required tools and techniques to get probable solution set. A judicious application of techniques and approaches keeping in view the socio-cultural environment has proved useful for achieving success. The practical experiences gained are inspiring.

November 2012 **Bholanath Das**

Acknowledgement

I am grateful to all my teachers and elders for their positive influence on my life for gaining knowledge. I would like to express gratitude to my family and my grandchildren (Geetikrisna, Baichitrinanda, Geetikriti, Poojashree, Bindusmita) who helped me in every stage of writing the book. I would like to acknowledge my inner guide to have shown me the path and inspiring all the way in my creative pursuit.

Many thanks are due to Dr. Lennart Sandholm (Stockholm University) for providing a deep insight in quality management as a subject of specialization. And last but not the least, I would like to thank my daughter Dr. Geeta and esteemed colleagues, Ms. Arpita Dey and Ms. Geetanjali Mohanty for their sincere help in the editing.

Abbreviations/Acronyms

APQP	Advance Product Quality Planning
AQL	Acceptable Quality Level
BIS	Bureau of Indian Standards
BIT	Built-in Test
BPR	Business Process Re-engineering
CAD	Computer Aided Design
CEDAC	Cause–and-Effect Diagram with the Addition of Cards
CMMI	Capability Maturity Model Integration
CWQC	Company Wide Quality Control
DfR	Design for Reliability
DIRFT	Doing It Right the First Time
DOX	Design of Experiment
EU	European Union
FMEA	Failure Mode and Effects Analysis
FRACAS	Failure Reporting, Analysis and Corrective Active Systems
ISI	Indian Standards Institute
ISO	International Organization for Standardization
JIT	Just-in-Time Manufacturing
JMA	Japanese Management Association
JUSE	Union of Japanese Scientists and Engineers
LCL	Lower Control limit
MSA	Measurement Systems Analysis
MTBF	Mean Time Between Failures
MTTR	Mean Time To Recovery
PDCA	Plan-Do-Check-Act
QA	Quality Assurance
QC	Quality Control
QCFI	Quality Circle Forum of India
QFD	Quality Function Deployment
QMS	Quality Management System
QSC	Quality Steering Committee
QWL	Quality of Work life

SPC	Statistical Process Control
SQC	Statistical Quality Control
SWOT	Strength and Weakness, Opportunity and Threat Analysis
TQ	Total Quality
TQC	Total Quality Control
TQM	Total Quality Management
UCL	Upper Control Limit
US	United States
USA	United States of America

1

Meaning, Characteristics and Importance of Quality

Quality is never an accident; it is always the result of intelligent effort. — John Ruskin

Development to date, most importantly technological and especially in the domain of computer and communication has transformed the social and economic fabric of the world, from business to education, habits to production. It tends to annihilate space and time, making one world a reality [1] and the opportunities created are enormous: business can expand horizon, exploit high growth potential in a borderless world; the consumers get advantage from the free movement of goods and services—unlimited choices, novel product features and competitive price. Alongside it has also introduced newer challenges; the producers, in particular, find the demand exacting, for the consumer perception and preferences are fast changing. Those enterprises which cope with the changing needs and accept 'survival of the fittest' are in a position to sustain in the competitive market environment and also grow when actively engage for achieving competitiveness in product and services.

Wilkinson *et al.* (1998) argues that 'the quest for quality is essentially a search for competitiveness'. [2] While price and availability once ruled, quality has emerged as one of the key success factors [3] over the past decades. Noted industrialist, Sir Henry Royce aptly observed, 'Quality is remembered long after price is forgotten'. And it is indeed amazing to look at the way industries in the entire developed economies including some developing countries have utilized quality as an instrument for business success and helped to gain economic prosperity.

Quality of products and services therefore assumes great importance for the manufacturers and must be reckoned with.

1.1 Quality Defined

The word 'quality' normally conveys notions primarily relating to aesthetic, the factors that are not readily measurable. This vague but nonetheless positive association makes the appeal of quality immediate, extensive, and universal. The earliest literature mentions of Aristotle to have analyzed quality in his logical work, *The Categories*. To him, qualities are hylomorphically formal attributes, such as 'white' or 'grammatical'. Categories of state, such as 'shod' and 'armed' are also non essential qualities *(katà symbebekós)*. Aristotle viewed quality as, 'one and the selfsame substance, while retaining its identity, is yet capable of admitting contrary qualities'.

For Locke, a quality is an idea of a sensation or a perception. Locke further asserts that qualities can be divided in two kinds: primary and secondary qualities. Primary qualities are intrinsic to an object, a thing or a person, whereas secondary qualities are dependent on the interpretation of the subjective mode and the aesthetic appearance.

While the above refers to philosophers' view of quality, product or service quality relates as much to the creation so much to the creator and the quality of a product in the final analysis is determined by the user from its functioning, safety and reliability including its aesthetics appeals. Essentially, quality is perceived to possess compelling values and is all about excellence and in the context of industry and business, it is imperative because quality is perhaps the only means that integrates the organization for achieving the set objective. [4]

'Quality relates not only to product and service but also includes process, environment and people', argues Uselac (1993: 20).

1.2 Characteristics of Quality

The defining characteristic of quality could be broadly grouped into subjective and objective. The subjective aspects conveying a perceptual, conditional and somewhat qualitative attributes are characteristics, or properties of a thing or phenomenon that can be observed and interpreted and may be approximated (quantified) but cannot be measured accurately, such as beauty, feel, flavour, taste including quality of work life (QWL), which is defined as 'the degree to which members of a work organization are able to satisfy important personal needs through their working experience in the organization'. [5] QWL, though subjective is now indexed through a standardized set of parameters in accordance with the evaluation methodology.

The objective parameters are measurable and verifiable. It is quantified and expressed in specific units of dimension in respect of the physical or chemical properties such as lightness or heaviness, thickness or thinness, softness or hardness and density to specific gravity. In manufacturing, it applies to the product specification based on the design standards and strict adherence is essential for achieving uniform output.

We deal with various aspects of quality continually in our daily lives, whether we articulate them openly or keep them in the back of our mind. Each one of us applies some of the many criteria even in a mundane instance like buying a dress from a store. Consider, for example, a situation—how a customer's perception finally influences his decision to buy or not to buy;

1. A customer enters the showroom—the ambience should be such that he is attracted.
2. The next step, how he is received—an inviting response engages him, or indifferent attitude distracts him.
3. Then he finds out whether the store offers a range that he could choose from.
4. The price tag, he mentally compares with the information he has and also considers some other aspects that may be important for him.

It is thus evident that the customer evaluates a number of factors in order to develop an overall perception that forms the basis for his decision. The store gains if it is able to meet or exceed the customer's expectation. As it is a representative business entity, the defining characteristics of quality essentially would relate not only to the product but to the whole organization: the process, environment and the people. It is thus all encompassing.

In practice too, quality assumes a wide variety of perceptions and interpretations for providing expression to a specific need: quality as 'conformance to standards' for the manufacturing industry sector, quality as 'excellence' for operators and supervisors at work place to take pride that their produce and also enjoy high esteem in the eyes of the customer, and so on.

In this context, Deming the distinguished quality expert credited with pioneering quality movement in the US and Japan presents an interesting insight, 'quality can be defined only in terms of the agent. Who is the judge of quality?' And he explains further, 'In the mind of the production worker, he produces quality if he can take pride in the work. Poor quality, to him, means loss of business and perhaps of his job. Good quality he thinks, will keep the company in business. Quality to the plant manager means to get the numbers out and to meet specifications. His job is also whether he knows it or not, continual improvement of leadership.' [6]

The workers and supervisors are concerned with quality of output, as they have been asked to produce, strictly meeting target and as per the design specification. This is necessary for a business processing unit, but not sufficient, because the ultimate judge of quality of a product is the user. The differentiation presents that the needs and preferences of a customer are the 'true quality' where as the quality of goods or services offered by producers' is 'internal quality'.

And manufacturers can attain success only when they pay more attention to 'true quality' rather than developing complacency on 'internal quality'. Deming also introduces an important dimension-continuous improvement of leadership in order to take care of the changing needs of customer, for quality is dynamic; it is ever changing, for customers may not consider today's product of good quality even acceptable tomorrow. The onus therefore lies on the management to orient improvement for accomplishing the goal.

1.3 Importance of Quality for Industry

The criticality of quality being 'customer satisfaction', the industry need to appreciate the importance of 'consumer preference and adjust the product to the public rather than, as in advertising, to adjust the public to the product' (Bross, 1993:95). Enhanced product quality and greater responsiveness to customers are no longer mere options for management, but are essential for survival in the present era of globalization. And importantly, 'outstanding quality generates satisfied customers who reward the organization with continued patronage and free word-of-mouth publicity'. [7]

The system for attaining and maintaining quality in industry is thus the imperative need. It has evolved over the years from the basic inspection by separating bad from the lot to managing total quality. The concept of 'total quality' combines almost all systems, sub-systems and processes in an enterprise that influences quality of output. It is an approach to doing business that attempts to maximize the competitiveness of an organization through the continual improvement of the quality of its products, services, people, processes and environment (Geotsch and David, 1994:6). Summing up, the 'total quality' approach would comprise:

1. Quality involves meeting customers' needs and preferences and exceeding it. In other words, it is 'customer focus'.
2. Quality applies not only to product and service, but encompasses people, process and environment.
3. Achieving quality in industry involves:

- Scientific approach to decision making and problem solving.
- Developing quality policy—clear vision, objective strategy, management commitment for continuous improvement, employees' empowerment, adopting modern management style to foster team work, enabling work environment, and last but not the least,
- Unity of purpose: company wide quality.

Total quality, therefore, is not simply limited to manufacture of product and services to specification, it is a whole new way of doing business. It entails managing systems and processes for the organization as a whole and involving all employees for attaining the organizational goal. And in the context of managing quality in industry, this is commonly described as 'Big Q' that refers to quality of product, service, people, process and system. [8]

The ultimate objective is developing an organization culture for successful operation of a company which can operate to the desired level and it is feasible only when:

1. It determines 'what customers need?' through market research,
2. It translates the 'customers requirements' to a quality product by innovative design, development and production,
3. It markets the product keeping in view the competitive market environment,
4. It ascertains whether the customers are satisfied through a system of feedback, and
5. It re-designs to suit the changing needs that meet their expectation through continuous improvement.

And the cycle continues.

While the systems and processes internal to the organization are important to achieve quality, the external factors too contribute. Of these, the suppliers and customers are the key determinants for a processing activity. In fact the contribution of suppliers and customers are equally vital in making products of good quality.

Figure 1.1: A Processing Model

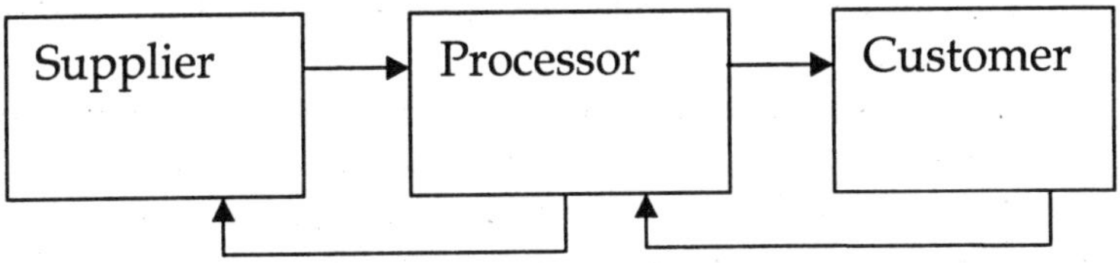

The schematic diagram presented in Figure 1.1 illustrates the inter-relationship of customer-processor and processor-supplier. It entails that an effective communication between customer-processor and supplier-processor is of paramount importance. A processor depends on suppliers to get inputs for making a product as the quality of input directly influences the quality of the output. The processor thus has to take action on:

1. Vendor evaluation and selection.
2. Informing vendors 'what is its requirements'.
3. Providing feedback not only regarding quantity, but also regarding the quality of supplies received including the areas where improvement is needed.

It is in addition to the usual discussion on price and delivery schedule.

The information would help the vendor to upgrade its system to cater to the demand of the processor and the processor in turn meets customer's requirement. Similarly, the processor-customer interaction is also very important. Receiving customer feedback regularly is crucial, for it is one of the important means to access the changing needs of the market. The company should develop a system for collecting customer re-action on the product and their views on other features that they would like in the product for evaluating these and incorporating the essential elements while redesigning the product.

A business organization can achieve the goal by properly

aligning its systems and processes, successfully transit to a total quality organization and establish quality culture. The total quality management promises to offer excellent solutions for most of the troubling business problems which the quality experts vouchsafe.

Quality being so critical to products and services, it is worth understanding what it is in its entirety-its evolution and definition to the present day quality management; why it is so important for business and industry; how to attain, maintain and manage quality of goods manufactured and services offered by the service providers and this book attempts to provide comprehensive insights in all these aspects.

End Notes

1. Das, Kamal in '*Managing Development*' describes the present world order as, 'a continued integration of world economy-a functioning world market, free trade, unimpaired movement of capital, technology, people, international division of labour and a comprehensive worldwide networking in 'real time'.
2. To Oakland (1993), 'quality is the most important of the competitive weapons'.
3. Critical Success Factor is an element of organizational activity which is central to its future success. It may change over time and may include items such as product quality, employee attitudes, manufacturing flexibility, and brand awareness.
4. 'Quality relates not only to product and service but also includes process, environment and people', argues Uselac (1993: 20).
5. J. Richard and J. Loy and Richard E. Walton takes a much broader concept of QWL proposing eight conceptual categories viz. adequate and fair compensation, safe and healthy working conditions, opportunity to use and develop human capacities, future opportunity for continued growth and security, social integration in the work place, social relevance of work, balanced role of work in the total life space and constitutionalism in the Work Organization etc. it is rare to find work-life situations that satisfy all eight criteria. We can view these eight features as goals to aim for.
6. Deming, W. E., '*Out of Crisis*' 1986: 158.
7. Frank Voehl, series editor in preface of Lindsay, William M. and

Joseph A. Petrick 'Total Quality and Organization Development' (1997:xii).

8. An obvious reference is made to 'Little Q' that focuses on the quality aspects of one or many of these elements concerning a specific department or work station in a business enterprise.

2

Evolution of the Concept of Quality

The recent decades witnessed greater concerns of the industry towards the need for improving quality and competitiveness of products and services. It is essentially due to emerging international competition—a natural outcome of the global development trends in the border-less world. By 1970s, the world was aware of the Japanese turnaround as its products took the industrialized Western economies by surprise: throwing open challenge to American manufacturers on its home turf. [1] The industries in the United States hurried to action with uneasy haste for implementing quality system that was considered crucial for survival and growth. [2] The enthusiasm for quality initiatives gradually assumed phenomenal proportion. It spread to most of the industrialized economies and some developing countries. The spurt in activities that bubbled up has since been smoothened to mature actions. The industry and business have also realized that managing quality is more and more indispensable as global business environment becomes more and more turbulent.

While the above presents post war experience, it would not be correct to assume that the concern for quality is of recent origin. In fact, it has been an age-old practice. The craft guilds of Middle Ages for example, considered creative work of quality as the deciding criteria for admittance to its membership—limiting to only those artisans who could achieve excellence in quality standards. Advanced civilizations too supported the creative arts and crafts, regarded skilled artisans with respect and encouraged clients to choose goods meeting higher quality standards than normal goods. The result is evident: the quality of craftsmanship in Egyptian pyramid to Indian temples epitomizes their skill and devotion to work.

The importance of craftsmen however diminished as industry adopted mass production and repetitive work practices. The need was to produce large numbers of the same goods. The first proponent in the US for this approach was Eli Whitney who introduced manufacture of interchangeable parts for muskets, hence producing the identical components and creating a musket assembly line. [3] The development that followed has been due to the imaginative application of scientific techniques at shop floor for increasing productivity. The creative practice was pioneered by Frederick Winslow Taylor, a mechanical engineer who sought to improve efficiency of workers especially in the manufacturing sector. He was one of the intellectual leaders of the Efficiency Movement and part of his approach laid a foundation for scientific management technique that includes standardization of working methods for production including adoption of improved practices. He gained acclaim as 'the father of scientific management.'

From this period onwards, companies in the industrially advanced countries focused predominantly on development and introduction of new methods for increasing productivity and efficiency in order to achieve lower cost of commodities to satisfy customers and stakeholders in the company.

2.1 Milestones in Quality Movement

Since early twentieth century the industry progressed with many technological advancements and innovations and alongside the need for quality of product became increasingly important. The development of a system for achieving quality of products has been due to the meaningful contribution of many men of wisdom. The quality management that evolved over the years as a scientific practice began from the concept of separating good product that conformed to design specification from the non-conforming items, termed as bad.

The important landmarks in the evolution of quality concepts from inspection through quality control, quality assurance to quality management covered under the broad canvas of 'total quality' include the following important events presented in Table 2.1.

Table 2.1: Landmark Events in Quality Management

Year	Landmark Events
1911	Frederick W. Taylor publishes '*The Principle of Scientific Management*'-the techniques for time and motion study.
1931	Walter A. Shewhart introduces statistical quality control in his book, '*Economic Control of Quality of Manufactured Products*'.
1940s	W. Edwards Deming develops a new quality philosophy.
1950s	W. Edwards Deming assists Japanese companies for introduction of quality practice at work place.
1951	Joseph M. Juran publishes '*Quality Control Handbook*'
1970	Philip B. Crosby applies the concept of 'Zero Defect'.
1979	Philip Crosby publishes '*Quality is Free*'.
1982	W. Edwards Deming publishes '*Quality, Productivity and competitive Position*'.
1987	US announces Malcolm Baldrige National Quality Award.
1990s	The total quality approach gains wide popularity in industry world over and courses on quality management offered in universities.

Prior to industrialization, attaining quality of product has been craftsman's responsibility which Feigenbaum refers to as 'operator quality control'. A highly skilled craftsman used to perform all tasks required-planning, procurement, production, quality control. In a sense, the craftsman was manager, worker, quality inspector all rolled into one. Industrial revolution ushered in a new era introducing mass production of goods that led to division of labour, specialization and many developments in the sphere of manufacturing technique as well as in quality control and management.

The modern quality control owes its origin to the system of production made in batches requiring inter-changeability of components and parts for subsequent assembly. [4] The origin of technical systems for industry is traced to the time and motion study conducted by Frederick Winslow Taylor in 1920s. He introduced the concept of scientific management for increasing productivity, differentiated planning and production functions: planning as the job of management and production—the job of workers. As the volume of production increased, it became necessary to create separate quality department, initially designated as 'inspection and quality control'. During the early phase of development, the result was far from satisfactory which could be attributed to the following reasons:

1. The operators and their supervisors lacked the basic education and knowledge regarding quality: what is quality and how it is to be attained and controlled. They were satisfied with the quantity of production that met targets.
2. The responsibility of achieving quality of product was vague and confused. The production supervisors tried to shift the responsibility to quality inspectors.
3. Senior management remained detached from the process of managing quality. They lacked understanding, considered quality a cost burden.

The system of quality control, quality assurance and quality management gradually developed due to the pioneering works of many distinguished experts in the field of quality. The contributions of Walter A. Shewhart, W. Edward Deming, Joseph M. Juran, Philip Crosby, Armand V. Feigenbaum and Kaoru Ishikawa among others merit discussion.

2.2 Walter Andrew Shewhart's Contribution

Shewhart was a brilliant thinker. While working with the inspection in Engineering Department at Hawthorne Works of the Western Electric Company in 1918, he felt constrained with the limited option of inspecting finished products and removing defective items. The volume of rejects and wastes generated during the manufacturing process of identical parts became his concern. To deal with the problem, he developed a system consisting three elements, viz.

1. The act of specifying what is required.
2. The act of producing that has been specified.
3. The act of measuring for conformance.

He realized that variation is pervasive and control of quality characteristics must be a matter of probability where statistical control may play an important role for attaining uniformity in the production process.

His innovative application of the theory of statistics to control the quality of products was the work of a master mind. The concept was written in the one page monograph of May 16, 1924. It contained a simple diagram which could be described today as a schematic control chart. That diagram and the short text which preceded and followed it, set forth all of the essential principles and considerations which are involved in process quality control and it became the new approach to quality control. Shewhart's work pointed out the importance of reducing variation in a manufacturing process because increased variation generally degraded quality of output and created non-conformance resulting in waste. [5]

He developed control charts by carefully designed experiments and set control limits on the basis of theory of Statistics. The set of data obtained by actual measurement of the samples taken randomly from the output are plotted on the control chart. The graphic presentation clearly displays the process variation which could be interpreted statistically as under:

1. The variation from the mean (centre line of the control chart) but within the control limits are natural to the process. The variances occur due to random or chance causes within the system. These are not of any concern to the production process and the process is in a state of statistical control.
2. The variation that goes beyond the control limits are due to assignable causes. It needs analysis for finding probable causes and solution so that the defects in the

manufacturing processes are rectified in order to bring the process under control.

These are used as a ready guide for suitable action, as and when required. The system is Statistical Quality Control (SQC) and Shewhart is rightly called the 'founding father of SQC'.

The result from the application of SQC overwhelmed the industry on account of the following:

1. The costly post production segregation was eliminated.
2. The total inspection was replaced by sampling.
3. Immediate prevention of problems and improvement of the process for minimizing waste.
4. The workers were at ease to stay within the tolerance limits rather than striving for unnecessary or unattainable perfection.

2.3 Quality Philosophy of Edwards Deming

W. Edwards Deming was greatly influenced by Shewhart's concept for controlling enormous waste generated at the plant. He carried forward the concept of statistical quality control and application of sampling technique in production and with his experience at Western Electric achieved the status of an internationally acclaimed quality expert. He has played the role of visionary, distilling disparate management ideas into a compelling new philosophy (Gabor, 1990:2). His important contributions to the quality movement are Deming Cycle, his 14 points and seven deadly diseases.

2.3.1 Deming Cycle: The Deming Cycle (also known as PDCA Cycle) focuses on cooperative effort of research, design, production, marketing in a firm to satisfy consumer needs. The Plan-Do-Check-Act (PDCA) cycle in practice means the following steps in a manufacturing concern:

1. Conduct consumer research and use the data in the design of the product (Plan).
2. Produce quality product (Do).
3. Measure for conformance (Check).

4. Market the product (Act).
5. Evaluate the performance at marketplace (Analyze).

2.3.2 Deming's Fourteen Points for Achieving Quality: The fourteen points that summarizes his philosophy for achieving quality in product and service are as follows:

1. Create constancy of purpose for improvement of product and services in order to stay in business. Research, innovation, continuous improvement is mandatory.
2. Adopt new philosophy-poor quality of product/service and bad attitude are unacceptable.
3. Cease dependence on mass production-reduction of waste in the process is necessary for cost control. New methods like 'lean manufacturing' has been developed in response to the emerging market demand.
4. End the practice of awarding business on price tag alone-lowest price concept is no longer valid. Long-term relationship with supplier ensuring quality and value of supplies are a must.
5. Improve the process constantly and forever-it is the responsibility of the management to continuously upgrade the quality of output to stay in business.
6. Institute training-the workers need to know the job they are to handle.
7. Institute leadership—selection of leaders with right aptitude from among the employees and training them.
8. Drive out fear—any change in product or process is seen by workers as threats. This is to be removed by education and proper communication.
9. Break down barriers between staff areas-team spirit is essential for success. A good leader can instil the spirit in employees.
10. Eliminate slogan, exhortation, targets for work force-develop organizational culture so that everyone is motivated to do the job willingly and achieve the organizational goal.
11. Eliminate numerical quotas—priority to shift from

quantity to quality output.

12. Remove barrier to pride of artisanship—encourage attaining excellence with reward for the deserving.
13. Institute education and training programme—every employee in the quality organization should learn quality concepts, systems, application of tools and techniques. The empowerment would result in willing participation for better performance.
14. Take action for smooth transition to new system—all from top to bottom should be involved. Their commitment to accomplishing the goal brings success.

2.3.3 Deming's Seven Deadly Diseases: Deming designates the following important aspects as 'seven deadly diseases' because these could be main causes for poor performance and often missed or ignored by the management:

1. Lack of constancy of purpose to plan product and service that will have a market and keep the company in business and provide jobs.
2. Emphasis on short-term profits: short term thinking, fed by fear of unfriendly takeover by bankers and owners, for dividends.
3. Personnel review system, or evaluation of performance, merit rating, annual review, or annual appraisal, by whatever name, for people in management, the effects of which are devastating. Management by objective would be better with a sense of accomplishment.
4. Mobility of management: job hopping.
5. Use of visible figures only for management, with little or no consideration of figures that are unknown or unknowable.
6. Excessive medical costs (excessive technology costs, security and operational expense).
7. Excessive costs of warranty, fuelled by lawyers' contingency fees.

While Deming's 'fourteen points' is the summary of his quality philosophy, the seven deadly diseases relate to the vital issues which the management should be concerned with in order to motivate people for better performance which eventually minimizes wastes and costs.

2.4 Joseph Juran's Approach

The important contributions of Joseph M. Juran [6] to quality philosophy are the Three Basic Steps to Progress, Ten Steps to Quality Improvement, The Pareto Principle and The Juran Trilogy. The salient features of each of these are explained below:

2.4.1 Juran's Three Basic Steps to Progress:

1. Achieve structured improvements on a continual basis combined with dedication and a sense of urgency.
2. Establish a system of extensive Training Programme.
3. Ensure commitment and leadership on the part of higher management.

2.4.2 Juran's Ten Steps to Quality Improvement

1. Build awareness of both the need for improvement and opportunity for improvement.
2. Set goals for improvement.
3. Organize to meet the goals that have been set.
4. Provide training.
5. Implement project aimed at solving problems.
6. Report progress.
7. Give recognition.
8. Communicate results.
9. Keep score.
10. Maintain momentum by building improvement into the company's regular system.

2.4.3 The Juran Trilogy: Juran in his paper 'The Quality Trilogy: a universal approach to managing quality' concludes that 'There is a crisis in quality. Our traditional ways are not adequate to deal with it and the companies need to chart a new direction in managing quality.' [7] He proposes a universal concept 'quality trilogy' which fits all functions, all levels, and all product lines. It consists of three basic management processes—quality planning, quality control and quality improvement. 'Each of these processes is universal; it is carried out by an unvarying sequence of activities.' he suggests.

1. The quality planning involves the following:
    - Determining who the customers (both external and internal) are?
    - Identifying their needs.
    - Designing product with features that respond to their needs.
    - Establishing quality goals that meet the needs of customers, suppliers and doing so at a minimum cost.
    - Developing process with capability to produce the required product features.
2. The quality control function relates to assessing actual performance by:
    - Choosing control subjects (what to control).
    - Developing standards of performance.
    - Deciding measurement system and measuring actual performance.
    - Comparing with the standard and interpreting the difference.
    - Taking action if the performance and goals differ.
3. The quality improvement aims at outperforming the past by reducing chronic level of quality deficiencies, project by project. It is a continuous process consisting of the following steps:
    - Identify specific project for improvement.
    - Establish project team with responsibility.
    - Provide resources needed for development of required infrastructure for quality improvement.
    - Diagnose to find the root causes.
    - Develop solutions for remedies.
    - Establish systems to maintain data with regard to the gains achieved.

The company managers should take up the new responsibilities-prepared for meeting the strategic goals that involve evaluation of competitive quality trends in the marketplace. Introduction of required changes in the basic steps in trilogy (quality planning, quality control and quality improvement) and conducting training for the personnel assigned to implement projects are essential prerequisite. It involves a shift in emphasis: from pure technology application to quality management, from only quality control to strategic quality planning. It is the wave of the future and those who accept and pursue the goal set accomplish. It is certainly an exhilarating experience to realize tangible gains: reducing defects from 25 percent level to 5 percent level within a period of one year. [8]

2.5 Vilfredo Pareto Principle

The principle is also called the 80/20 rule: 80 percent of the trouble comes from 20 percent of the problem. Though named after the noted economist Vilfredo Pareto, Juran applied the idea to managing quality problems. His advice is to concentrate on the 'vital few' sources of problem and not distracted by those of lesser importance. [9]

2.6 Philip Bayard Crosby's Contribution

Crosby with his corporate experience at ITT formed Philip Crosby Associates-a quality consulting firm until 1992. His response to the quality crisis was the principle of 'doing it right the first time' (DIRFT) [10] In addition, he also introduced the concept of 'zero-defect' and steps for quality improvement. The important concepts introduced by him to quality concepts are the following:

2.6.1 Four Absolutes: His quality management philosophy could be summarized as four absolutes:

1. The definition of quality is conformance to requirement.
2. The system of quality is prevention of problems.
3. The performance standard of quality is zero defects.

4. The measurement of quality is the price of non-conformance, or the cost of quality.

2.6.2 Zero-defect: He emerged as a quality expert with his 'zero-defect' concept in the manufacturing. In addition, Crosby's Quality Vaccine comprises three components, viz. (a) determination, (b) education, and (c) implementation.

2.6.3 Fourteen Steps: Crosby's fourteen steps to quality improvement programme suggest an all encompassing measures and comprise:

1. Management is committed to quality—and this is clear to all.
2. Create quality improvement teams—with (senior) representatives from all departments.
3. Measure processes to determine current and potential quality issues.
4. Calculate the cost of (poor) quality.
5. Raise quality awareness of all employees.
6. Take action to correct quality issues.
7. Monitor progress of quality improvement—establish a zero defects committee.
8. Train supervisors in quality improvement.
9. Hold 'zero defects' days.
10. Encourage employees to create their own quality improvement goals.
11. Encourage employee communication with management about obstacles to quality.
12. Recognise participants' effort.
13. Create quality councils.
14. Do it all over again—quality improvement does not end.

2.7 Kaoru Ishikawa: The Japanese Expert

As the president of Union of Japanese Scientists and Engineers (JUSE) in 1960s, Kaoru Ishikawa has been responsible for development of quality systems in Japan. He translated, integrated and expanded the management concepts of Deming and Juran into the Japanese system and enriched the quality field by developing certain unique strategies for achieving quality in manufactured products and the important among them are 'quality circle' and 'cause-and-effect diagram'.

1. He introduced a novel approach to form quality circle and with his initiative and skill, he could mobilize large groups of people to work towards the common organizational goal.
2. It is to a large extent considered crucial for achieving quality improvement in Japanese industry.
3. The 'cause-and-effect diagram' also called 'fishbone diagram' is a very useful tool for analyzing and identifying root cause of many quality problems. It helps to find a probable solution set so in order to eliminate chronic problems and bringing the process under control.
4. He also stressed the need for top management to assume leadership role for implementation of quality management as a policy, pursuing open communication with clear objective and operating guidelines.
5. He identified the following seven factors critical for successful implementation of total quality system in a business organization:
    - Participation of all employees of the organization for successful implementation of company-wide quality.
    - Education and training of employees on quality concepts, tools and techniques.
    - Participation in quality circle.
    - Quality audits by senior management twice a year.
    - Application of relevant tools and technique for identification of causes for prevention and elimination.
    - Nationwide promotion of quality control in industry.
    - Proactive attitude of management and workers towards customers and continuous improvement.

2.8 Armand Feigenbaum

Armand Feigenbaum worked as vice president of worldwide quality for General Electric until late 1960s and then setup his quality consulting firm. In his pioneering book, '*Total Quality Control*' he advocates integration of man-machine-information structure for effectively controlling quality and achieve customer satisfaction. He uses the concept of 9Ms—the nine factors that affect quality: market, money, management, men, motivation, materials and machines including mechanization, modern information system and mounting product requirements. Andrea Gabor (1990) notes that 'his focus on 'nuts and bolt' approach benefited the industry during 1970s and 1980s in quality improvement'.

His systems theory of total quality control consists of four fundamental principles:

1. Total quality is a continuous process, starting with customer requirement and ending with customer satisfaction.
2. Documentation allows visualization and proper communication of work to be done.
3. Quality system provides flexibility, because of alternative approaches.
4. Systematic re-engineering of quality activities leads to continuous improvement.

2.9 Quality in Industry

The Great Britain ruled supreme in maritime trade during colonial era and from the early twentieth century the United States and some European countries tried to consolidate their position with economic progress and military prowess. While expansionism led to two world wars during the first half of twentieth century, it accelerated the pace of industrial and technological development for meeting wartime requirement. In the manufacturing sector, Henry Ford introduced automatic production machines, assembly lines and methods of measurement to control quality of the outputs. In Germany, Karl Friedrich Benz often called the inventor of the motor car, was pursuing similar assembly and production practices.

2.9.1 Wartime Developments: This period witnessed spurt in demands in respect of weapons, means of transport and in order to meet the demand, industry introduced mass production which created scope for workmen to earn more by producing extra quantity which in turn led to bad workmanship as some of the parts did not conform to specification and passed on to subsequent manufacturing stages in the assembly lines.

In order to control the poor quality of products, full time inspectors were introduced in the factory to identify, quarantine and ideally correct product quality failures. Quality control by inspection up to the 1920s was based on quality inspection functions primarily to separate non-conforming parts from total output. Quality control department headed by superintendents formed part of the organization structure. The notable developments during the war, especially in respect of industry include faster technological advancement, improvement in methods of production process; that is, manufacturing large volume in short notice and control of quality by inspection to ensure that the products do not fail during use.

Walter A. Shewhart made a major step in the evolution of quality system. He innovatively applied the concepts of statistics and created a novel method for the control of product quality. It was also described as Statistical Quality Control (SQC). The first application of SQC was at Bell Laboratories in 1924 for controlling production process to get quality output and this is considered as one of the most effective tools in industry world over even to date. The concept of SQC relied on the fact that a total batch of products should not be fully inspected for ensuring quality, for in certain cases 100 percent inspection is not feasible and in general it is uneconomical. The technique employs a system of sampling for measurement by inspection and the data plotted in the control charts are interpreted for corrective action, as required.

Shewhart viewed that all manufacturing processes are inherently variable and process variability is random. And as long as the variation in the output is within the specified limits, the product conforms to the standard; failing which there is need for investigation for rectification. The measurement of the critical parameters forms the basis to determine whether the variation in the process is within control limits or out of it that requires attention. Standard statistical techniques allow the producer to sample and measure a certain proportion of the products for conformance to quality specification in order to achieve the desired level of confidence in the quality of the entire batch or production run. The control charts designed and developed in Bell Laboratories in the 1930s are the process control charts and being used to monitor process output in industry.

W. Edwards Deming applied statistical process control methods in the United States during World War II, thereby successfully improving quality in the manufacture of munitions and other strategically important products. And following the world war, the United States emerged as the undisputed world leader in commerce and industry.

2.9.2 Post-War Developments: While a few manufacturing concerns adopted SQC for quality control, for majority of manufacturers the central activity of the quality department continued to be inspection and it became a habit for the industry. The benefit of such activity was limited to very short-term, by reducing the risk that defective products do not reach customer and defective parts do not enter into the next stage of production.

The organization structure however has serious detriments: the centralized activity of the quality department helped to foster a wide spread belief that achievement of quality was the sole responsibility of the quality department. In turn, it could not encourage efforts at eliminating causes of the defective production process, operator's shortcomings, or deficiency in other inputs. The responsibilities were confused. 'As a result, the failure prone products and incapable processes remained in force and continued to generate high cost, poor quality output' comments Juran in *'Juran on Leadership for Quality'* (1989:6).

Gradually, the quality control approach developed into a system of statistical method of quality control to begin with. [11] It initiated a trend to effectively use quality, moving away from traditional after-the–fact approach to incorporating quality in design and during production. The 'quality engineering' of 1930s also developed into a new branch in the 1950s, designated as the 'reliability engineering'. It aims at achieving functional efficiency in products.

2.10 Reliability Engineering

A systemic definition of reliability is 'the ability of a person, product or system to perform and maintain its functions in routine circumstances, as well as in hostile or unexpected circumstances'. Reliability in respect of manufacturing process refers to reliability engineering, which is the ability of a system or component to perform its required functions under stated conditions for a specified period of time. Technically, functional efficiency is achievable if taken care of at the design stage, that is, by designing reliability into products, deploying quality tools and scientific techniques for process control.

2.10.1 Design for Reliability: The first step in the design for reliability (DFR) process is to set the system's reliability requirements and allocating the top-level reliability requirements to subsystems by design engineers and reliability engineers working together. Reliability design begins with the development of a reliability model using block diagrams and fault trees to provide a graphical means of evaluating the relationships between subsystems and the system. These models incorporate predictions based on the failure rates taken from historical data. While the predictions are often not accurate in an absolute sense, they are valuable inputs to assess relative differences in design alternatives. Some of the most important design techniques are redundancy, physics of failure and component de-rating.

2.11 Redundancy

It involves providing additionally an alternative to take care of expected functions of a part or equipment in the event of failure of the original, that is, if one part of the system fails, there is an alternate success path, such as a backup system. For example, an automobile brake light uses two light bulbs. If one bulb fails, the brake light still operates using the other bulb. Redundancy significantly increases system reliability and is often an easy, safe and viable means of doing so. But it is expensive. Thus, its application is normally limited to critical parts of the system.

2.12 Physics of Failure

The method relies on understanding the physical processes of stress, strength and failure at a very detailed level. Then the material or component can be re-designed to reduce the probability of failure. It requires intensive research and development.

2.13 Component De-rating

It is another common design technique. Selecting components whose capacity significantly exceeds the expected stress, as using a heavier gauge wire that exceeds the normal specification.

In addition, the other commonly used techniques and analyses that find application to specific product or industry include:

1. Built-in test (BIT).
2. Failure Mode and Effect Analysis (FMEA).
3. Reliability Simulation Modelling.
4. Reliability Block Diagram Analysis.
5. Thermal Tests and Analysis.
6. Sneak Circuit Analysis.
7. Fault Tree Analysis.
8. Accelerated Testing.
9. Reliability Growth Analysis.

10. Weibull Analysis.
11. Electromagnetic analysis.

It is however to be noted that reliability is just one requirement among many system requirements and an optimum balance amongst the reliability and other requirements and constraints are decided during the evaluation of preliminary design phase keeping in view the product quality in order to meet customer satisfaction.

2.14 Reliability Sequential Test Plan

The purpose of reliability testing is to discover potential problems with the design as early as possible and, ultimately, provide confidence that the system meets its reliability requirements. Reliability testing may be performed at several levels. Complex systems may be tested at component, subassembly, assembly, subsystem and system levels. Testing proceeds during each level of integration through full-up system testing, developmental testing, and operational testing, thereby reducing programme risk. System reliability is calculated at each test level. Reliability growth techniques—failure reporting, analysis and corrective active systems (FRACAS) are often employed to improve reliability as testing progresses. The limitations for such extensive testing is time and cost.

As part of the initial decision, the reliability engineer develops a test strategy with the customer. The test strategy is essentially a trade-off between the needs of the reliability data as much as possible and constraints such as expense and available resources. Test plans and procedures are developed for each reliability test and results are documented in the official reports. Most of the quality organizations maintain a data structure and the data are constantly analyzed using statistical techniques.

A system of surveillance of critical parameters identified during the fault tree analysis at design stage is introduced which is monitored and assessed by reliability engineers for correcting deficiencies noted. In the event of large field upgrades or recall repairs, additional reliability testing is required for design changes to ensure reliability. It is seen that manufacturing organizations are adopting this method and utilizing in commercial systems such as a Web based FRACAS application to create a failure/incident data repository from which statistics can be derived to view accurate and genuine reliability, safety and quality performances.

Some of the common outputs from a FRACAS system includes: Mean Time Between Failures (MTBF), Mean Time to Recovery (MTTR) or response time, Spares Consumption, Reliability Growth, Failure/Incidents distribution by type, location, part no., serial no, symptom etc. While for small, non-critical systems, reliability engineering may be informal, as complexity grows, the need arises for a formal reliability function. Because reliability is important to the customer, the customer may even specify certain aspects of the reliability organization. It is however to be appreciated that failures do occur, since it is not possible to anticipate all the failure modes of a given system, especially ones involving human element. It is however possible to reduce it to minimum. If not eliminating altogether, by proper design techniques, discussed above.

2.15 Quality Improvement in Japan

During the War, the world witnessed an accelerated pace of industrial and technological development. Alongside, distinguished quality experts like Deming and Juran developed innovative quality concepts and strategies for improving product quality and reducing controllable costs. Post-War, the industry in the United States did not pay attention to these developments. Consequently the American consultants found favourable environment for implementing their ideas in Japan because the war torn country, in its quest to rebuild the economy launched massive programme to learn how to improve product quality and compete in the international market.

Japan borrowed technology including quality management concept, methods, tools and techniques from the West, particularly the United States, blended it with its own ideas to suit its socio-cultural ethos and tailored approaches for quality improvement enlisting employees' co-operation and participation. The professionals involved in the process of transformation also developed some new approaches, new tools and techniques and the important among the new tools and techniques that enriched the quality practice include:

1. Quality Circle that led to *Kaizen*—a system of continuous improvement.
2. Specialized tools and techniques like Fish-bone diagram, Just-in-Time developed by Ishikawa, Ohno among others.
3. The Toyota Production System for achieving total quality at reduced cost.

The stunning success achieved by Japanese industry simply overwhelmed the world, particularly the western industries. By 1970s, Japan began to challenge the United States with its products in the important sectors like automobiles and consumer electronics. And by 1980s, Japan emerged as an economic power, competing American products for which it borrowed technology from the US. Juran describes the turnaround of Japanese industry as, 'To solve their quality problems, the Japanese undertook to learn how other countries managed for achieving quality. To this end the Japanese sent teams abroad to visit foreign companies and study their approach. They translated selected foreign literature into Japanese. They also invited foreign lecturers to come to Japan and conduct training courses for managers.' The strategies developed in Japan that brought about a revolution in quality have been unprecedented and most of these were decisive. The novel practices that other industries could emulate include the following:

1. The upper management personally took charge of leading the revolution.

2. All levels and functions underwent training in managing for quality.
3. Quality improvement was continuous.
4. The workforce participated in quality improvement through Quality circle concept' (Juran, 1989:7-8).

The Japanese miracle was due to the concerted effort of industry with the support of government, scientists, economists and technologists who subordinated everything to the organization and there by to the nation.

The impact was felt by the developed economies. The industrially advanced countries in the West, especially the United States found losing their market share. America, at first reacted with restrictive legislation like higher duty and quota on imports, but there was no tangible success. Bright, talented and determined people engaged in managing industry worked to reverse the erosion of country's market share but of no avail. The situation is aptly described as, 'American managers have traditionally been well versed in the production, marketing, financial aspects, management information system and quantitative aspects of their world.

Many managers, who have excellent conceptual and technical skills, tend to be inadequately prepared in people skill and technical process skills. They seem to have a difficult time leading people to work together toward the mission of the organization. The most significant problem is the lack of commitment to the organizational, managerial and logistical changes that must occur in order to become or remain competitive' (Uselac, 1993:4). They began to realize that the key to competing in global marketplace was to improve overall quality.

The point made is that excellence in production, marketing, finance and quantitative aspects are necessary but not sufficient. It is equally essential that the managers should have competence in managing people, developing and improving process with proper design for quality. And in order to enlist employee's unqualified involvement, empowerment was a necessity. It involved properly designed training to improving their knowledge and skills for getting quality output.

The rationale is simple: ensuring product/service quality is to continually improve people, process and environment through the implementation of total quality system. It is perhaps the best and effective way to survive and grow in the era of global competition. 'The 20th century will be remembered as the Century of Productivity, whereas the 21st century will come to be known as the Century of Quality.' so predicted Joseph M. Juran, while offering consultancy in quality movement for Japanese industry. [12]

2.16 Quality Consciousness in India

Independent India decided with overwhelming majority to pursue a policy for achieving self reliance. The industry, trade, foreign collaboration and investment policies were restrictive. The industries operated in a sellers' paradise for decades. Under compelling circumstances, the early 1990s witnessed a paradigm shift: a closed inward-looking policy regime changing to open trade and investment policy by repealing restrictive import control orders, reducing tariff on imports, inviting foreign direct investment.

Consequent to economic liberalization, the manufacturers and service providers are in search of new avenues to sustain in the market in the face of international competition. Inspired by the fast economic progress of the East Asian countries including China, Indian enterprises too became keen to chart the proven path: emulate models and strategies for success. And quality has emerged a key parameter to manage for development.

Thus programme on quality improvement gained momentum. A large number of self proclaimed experts, consultants like Lawrence, Curleigh and Mough [13] appeared in the scene with programmes for quality improvement including ISO certification, training for quality practice in industry and the like. The expected change for the better seems to be happening, but at a slow pace and in isolated pockets. A number of factors are attributed to hamstring positive outcome and the important among these are:

1. India's experience in industrial development is limited and for quite sometime it has been without much competition.
2. The traditionalism, public sector culture continues as the inertia still hangs on.
3. A large number of small and medium sector firms offer a wide range of products and services but have serious resource limitations by way of capital, technology and managerial.

Theoretically, small firms should offer better opportunity for managing change because they operate in a flexible social setting and have harmonious working relationship that offers better scope to resolve conflict for unanimity. In fact, the situation in India is to the contrary: units managed by proprietors who generally are autocratic in style could hardly succeed in creating an environment conducive to motivation for realizing the organizational goal.

In addition, most of the small firms have many other shortcomings—they do not have adequate professional support for developing proper strategy, do not draw any long-term plan and run day-to-day business on informed rationalization, lack resource. On the other end, the large corporations, particularly the public sector companies exhibit diverse sub-cultures and find difficult to develop quality culture in the organization. The story on the quality front is therefore astonishingly disappointing.

The situation has to change. A new management approach for implementing quality improvement seems imperative. Open trade has introduced competition; the trade and industry must accept that business would prosper only when it is oriented to customer satisfying process rather than limiting to goods and services produced and delivered. The emerging market environment is set to induce the industry for establishing quality culture, in its own interest though it may take some more time.

End Notes

1. Lindsay and Petrick in *'Total Quality and Organization Development'* note that 'Japanese firms have used many different resources to achieve their stunning victories, but excellent HRM policies and practices, supportive organization structures and an effective educational infrastructure have been contributing factors to their success and challenge to U S'.
2. Ford Motor Company invited Deming to start quality initiative when they realized that their market share was on the decline.
3. The real mass production was properly initiated in Volkswagen after World War II.
4. Stewart's pioneering text '*Economic Control of Quality of Manufactured Products*' is viewed as a landmark in the development of a system of quality management.
5. Shewhart's work is summarized in his book '*Economic Control of Quality of Manufactured Product*', 1931.
6. His Juran Institute Inc. in Wilton, Connecticut is internationally recognized for conducting training, research and consulting in quality management.
7. Juran, J. M., '*The Quality Trilogy: a universal approach to managing quality*' Quality Progress, August, 1986:19.
8. The experience of quality improvement programme at Electrolux: reduced wastage from US$ 3.8 million to US$ 0.5 million within a year.
9. Juran also points out that 'at least 85 percent of the problems can only be corrected by changing systems (management responsibility) and less than 15 percent are under the worker's control-and the split may lean even more towards the system'.
10. Crosby has broadened his approach to include wider improvement ideals. He also defines the five characteristics of an 'Eternally Successful Organisation' as: (i) People routinely do things right first time, (ii) Change is anticipated and used to advantage, (iii) Growth is consistent and profitable, (iv) New products and services appear when needed, and (v) Everyone is happy to work there.
11. Juran in 'Juran on Leadership for Quality' writes on quality engineering, 'This specialty traces its origin to the application of

statistical methods for control of quality in manufacture. Much of the pioneering theoretical work was done in 1920s by the quality assurance department of the Bell Telephone Laboratories. The staff members included Shewhart, Dodge and Edwards. Much of the pioneering application took place within the Hawthorn works of Western Electric Company'.

12. De Feo, Joseph A. *'The Future Impact of Quality'* Quality Engineering, Marcel Dekker, Volume 13, Number 3, 2001.
13. Townsend and Gebhardt in *'Quality in Action'* offer an interesting narration, p. 1.

3

Quality, Standards and ISO Certification

3.1 Various Definitions of Quality

Quality is an unusually slippery concept, easy to visualize and yet exasperatingly difficult to define (Garvin, 1988:ix). Even after its application to products for about a century, its connotation remains qualitative and subjective. There is little agreement on what constitutes quality. In its broader sense, however quality is an important attribute of a product or service that reflects value for money for a customer or user. It is a measure of excellence or state of being free from defects, deficiencies and significant variations. Anyone who treats quality as a solely rational exercise, misses an essential truth. Quality is not only cerebral, it is emotional; it touches both the heart and the head (Townsend and Gebhardt, 1992:ix).

Quality presents a dynamic state. It is not only associated with products, services, but also includes people, processes and environment (Uselac, 1993:20). The customer's perception of quality is also ever changing. The common element of the business definitions however refers to the perception of the degree to which the product or service meets the customer's expectations. Some important meanings assigned to quality by eminent personalities and institutions may offer an insight to the vast diversity quality seems to encompass. An elucidation follows:

1. **W. Edwards Deming:** Deming never defined quality precisely. To him, 'a product or a service possesses quality if it helps somebody and enjoys a good and sustainable market' and concentrates on 'the efficient production of the quality that the market expects'. He linked quality and management: 'costs go down and productivity goes up as

improvement of quality is accomplished by better management of design, engineering, testing and by improvement of processes.'

2. **Joseph M. Juran:** Juran asserts that the core content of quality is 'Fitness for use' and fitness is defined by the customer.
3. **Philip B. Crosby:** Crosby views quality as 'conformance to standards, specification, or requirements.' The requirements may not fully represent customer expectations. He treats this as a separate problem.
4. **Peter Drucker:** 'Quality in a product or service is not what the supplier puts in. It is what the customer gets out and is willing to pay for.'
5. **Genichi Taguchi:** offers two definitions, viz.

- 'Uniformity around a target value'—the idea is to lower the standard deviation in outcomes and to keep the range of outcomes to a certain number of standard deviations, with rare exceptions.
- 'The loss a product imposes on society after it is shipped'—this definition of quality is based on a more comprehensive view of the production system.

6. **Peters and Waterman:** Peters considers 'Quality as excellence' and more prosaically as 'delighting the customer'.
7. **Noriaki Kano and Others:** They present a two-dimensional model of quality: 'must-be quality' and 'attractive quality'. The former is near to 'fitness for use' and the latter is what the customer would love, but has not yet thought about. Supporters characterize this model more succinctly as: Products and services that meet or exceed customers' expectations.
8. **American Society for Quality:** It is a subjective term for which each person has his or her own definition. In technical usage, quality can have two meanings:

- The totality of features and characteristics of a product or service that bear on its ability to satisfy stated or implied needs;

- A product or service free of deficiencies.

9. **US Department of Defense:** It defines quality as 'doing the right thing right the first time, always striving for improvement and always satisfying customers'.
   The totality of features and characteristics of a product or service that bear on its ability to satisfy stated or implied needs.
10. **ISO 8402-1986, 3.1:** The international standard states quality as 'the totality of features and characteristics of a product or service that bears its ability to satisfy stated or implied needs.'
11. **ISO 9000:** It states, 'Degree to which a set of inherent characteristics fulfils requirements.' The standard defines *requirement* as need or expectation.

The salient features of product and service quality would broadly include the following.

3.2 Characteristics of Quality of Manufactured Products

Overall perception of quality is more of a subjective assessment of user but very important as the company may get a free word of mouth advertising.

1. Product aesthetics provides the first impression to a customer by its features, look, feel and appeal.
2. Performance is more important as it would generate customer satisfaction and continued patronage.
3. Conformance—the extent to which a product's characteristics match the stated parameters.
4. Safety—the product must be safe during use to the user.
5. Reliability—the time span a product continue to function to the satisfaction of a user,
6. Durability—how long user gets service before it calls for replacement.
7. Serviceability—the ease of repair and maintenance.

3.3 Dimensions of Quality in Services

1. Timeliness-does a service perform when needed?

2. Completeness—is the service complete in all respect for the required performance?
3. Consistency—is the service offered same at all time?
4. Accessibility—is it easy to obtain?
5. Accuracy—does the service perform right the first time?
6. Responsiveness—does the service provider resolve problems, if any?
7. User perception—an overall judgment that decides his/her continued patronage.

3.4 Quality Standards

The advent of machines for larger volumes of production of identical parts/components and assembly line to make a final product led to defining specification of each item of manufacture as per the design: the operators to produce as per specification, quality personnel to monitor that the output and process are within tolerance limits and customers to satisfy with their requirement. In order to achieve this, the manufacturing company provides a written document for all concerned to adhere to. This in-company design specification for the product is called 'company standard'.

The number of manufacturer of an item in a country gradually increased to meet the demand and it necessitated the development of 'national standard'. Standards of product and service for manufacture, usage and supply points have been playing a very important role in the industrial development. The manufacturers however are not compelled to adhere to the national standard and specification, except where human safety is involved.

The process began in Great Britain in early twentieth century and it was the only country engaged in developing national standard of products until 1915. By 1932, there were 25 countries having standardization organizations including the United States establishing an institution in 1917. The Indian Standards Institute (ISI) was created in independent India to take care the standardization function in line with industrialized countries. The ISI has since been renamed as Bureau of Indian Standards (BIS).

And of the many influencing developments in international trade, business the single most important features is globalization- a single global market place where any company from any country can participate on a platform and compete as per its competitive advantage. In such a scenario, national standard is found inadequate and a uniform standard for all players is considered imperative and international standard has become the order of the day for products and services. These standards are developed under the aegis of the International Organization for Standards [1] (ISO) with its headquarters at Geneva. It develops standards for conformance to quality of manufactured goods and services since 1987. In fact, international and national standards are now in use in over 160 countries which form the foundation of an effective Quality Management System (QMS).

The Quality Management System standards accepted by ISO are meant to certify the processes and the system of an organization, not the product or service itself. Specifically, the standard integrates the following eight quality management principles into its requirements:

1. Customer focus.
2. Leadership.
3. Involvement of people.
4. Process approach.
5. System approach to management.
6. Continual improvement.
7. Factual approach to decision-making.
8. Mutually beneficial supplier-customer relationships.

3.5 Process of Developing International Standard

A standardized system is followed for the development of international standards. Technical committees are formed with representation of international organizations, both government and non-government to prepare the draft on the topics of universal interest. It is circulated to member countries for their comments within a definite time frame. It is then deliberated upon in details and finalized. The standards are based on the quality system principles and quality system operations elements. ISO standards do not certify the quality of the product or service. The accepted standards are subject to review every few years by the ISO. It is a normal practice and a definite system exists for consideration, review and acceptance of a revised standard by standing technical committees and advisory groups, who receive feedback from member countries including professionals implementing the standard.

ISO 9004-1987, 0.4.5 states clearly that 'An effective quality management system should be designed to satisfy customer needs and expectations while serving to protect the company's interests. A well structured quality system is valuable management resource in the optimization and control of quality in relation to risk, cost and benefit consideration.'

ISO 9000 series are the basic document for quality system for use by companies as guideline to establish quality management system in the organization. The ISO 9000:1987 series of standards comprised ISO 9001:1987, ISO 9002:1987 and ISO 9003:1987, which were applicable in different types of industries, based on the type of activity or process: quality systems model for quality assurance in design, development, production and installation. For example:

1. ISO 9001-1987, 4.17 requires the quality organization to undertake comprehensive and regular review to determine that its quality activities comply with defined policies and practices.
2. The responsibility, authority and interrelationship of all personnel who manage, perform and verify work affecting quality shall be defined—ISO 9001-1987, 4.1.2.1.
3. Business should organize itself in such a way that the technical, administrative and human factors affecting the quality of its products and services will be under control.

All such control should be oriented towards the reduction, elimination and, most importantly, prevention of quality deficiencies (ISO 9004-1987, 0.2).

4. The organizational structure pertaining to the quality management system should be clearly established within the overall management of the company. The level of authority and communication should be defined (ISO 9004-1987, 5.2.3).

The standards relating to quality management system were developed in 1987 and reviewed and revised thrice—1994, 2000 and 2008.

1. The version approved in 1994 was called the ISO 9000:1994 series; comprising of the ISO 9001:1994, 9002:1994 and 9003:1994 versions.
2. The ISO 900: 2000 document gives guidelines for performance improvement over and above the basic standard (ISO 9001:2000). This standard provides a measurement framework for improved quality management, similar to and based upon the measurement framework for process assessment.
3. The last major revision was in the year 2008 and the series was called ISO 9000: 2008 series. The ISO 9002 and 9003 standards were integrated into one single certifiable standard: ISO 9001:2008.

ISO released a minor revision, ISO 9001:2008 on 14 October 2008. It contains no new requirements. Many of the changes were to improve consistency in grammar, facilitating translation of the standard into other languages for use by over 950,000 certified organizations in the 175 countries (as at December 2007) that use the standard. After December 2003, organizations holding ISO 9002 or 9003 standards had to complete a transition to the new standard.

In the context that the pursuit of product quality requires an organization to develop proper systems, the ISO 9001:2000 quality management system (QMS) is an internationally established quality framework. A systematic and independent examination to determine whether the quality activities and related results comply with planned arrangements and whether these arrangements are implemented effectively and are suitable to achieve objective (ISO 8402-1986, 3.10).

India has adopted these standards in its national standard and IS 10201 series is the equivalent of ISO 9000 series. Standards in India are developed under the aegis of Bureau of Indian Standards (BIS)—the institution responsible for the development of national standard. In India, many companies preferred to follow their own standard except where it is mandatory to follow national standard by statute. Such decision by the companies has been influenced by the fact that most of these companies manufacture with foreign technology support, follow the design of the technology supplier and any change involves large efforts including cost of design modification to production tooling and additional testing prior to acceptance.

3.6 Quality Management System

In terms of ISO 9001-2000, 3.2.3, the characteristics of a QMS in regard to quality include the following:

1. The establishment of policy and objectives by an organization to manage resources.
2. The assignment of responsibilities and authority to personnel.
3. The development of an organizational structure among the personnel.

It is also necessary to understand the equivalency between continuous and continual improvement so that we can readily use the terms interchangeably.

The normative definition in ISO 9000:2000 for continual improvement states that it is a recurring activity to increase the ability to fulfil requirements (3.1.2) The definition notes that the process (3.4.1) of establishing objectives and finding opportunities for improvement is a continual process through the use of audit findings (3.9.5) and audit conclusions (3.9.6), analysis of data, management reviews (3.8.7), or other means and generally leads to corrective action (3.6.5) or preventive action (3.6.4).

The standard provides the framework in which top management places its unified business plans, marketing, and sales promotions and strategies, establishes performance metrics, and records progress against goals to measure the effectiveness of the QMS. This is basically the plan-do-check/study-act scenario that was originally described as PDCA cycle by the American quality expert Walter A. Shewhart in 1931.

Plan basically comprises of following activity:

1. Quality policy.
2. Quality management system planning.
3. Planning for product realization.
4. Design and development planning.
5. Control of production and service provision.
6. General (measurement, analysis, and improvement).

The following standard paragraphs establish the *do* (implementation) protocols within which a company designs, manufactures and services its products:

1. General requirements.
2. General (documentation requirements).
3. Quality manual.
4. Control of documents.
5. Control of records.
6. Management commitment.
7. Customer focus.
8. Quality objectives.
9. Responsibility and authority.
10. Management representative.
11. Internal communication.
12. Provision of resources.
13. Human resources.
14. Infrastructure.
15. Work environment.

Determination of requirements related to the product or service for continuous improvement:

1. Review of requirements related to the product.
2. Customer communication.
3. Design and development inputs.
4. Design and development outputs.
5. Purchasing.
6. Identification and traceability.
7. Customer property.
8. Preservation of product.
9. Control of monitoring and measuring devices.
10. Monitoring and measurement of product.
11. Corrective action (w/response to customer complaints).
12. Preventive action.

Under *check/study*, the standard also provides for the mechanisms whereby we monitor our progress against quality goals so that the entire QMS can be analyzed and corrected to achieve continual improvement:

1. Management review.
2. Design and development verification.
3. Design and development validation.
4. Validation of processes for production and service provision.
5. Customer satisfaction.
6. Internal audit.
7. Analysis of data.

The *act* provision in the standard relates to establishing the methods required to correct those areas that are out of conformance for a long-term preventive action program. It includes the following:

1. Design and development review.
2. Control of design and development changes.
3. Monitoring and measurement of processes.
4. Control of non-conforming product.

There is operational power when all clauses are implemented. Thus, when all important elements of the standard are implemented, the paradigm ensures that the system will be documented; that those documents will be used by the employees; and that there will be adequate measurements made to judge whether or not we have demonstrated effective performance against our business/ quality objectives.

3.7 Industry Specific Standards

In 2005 the International Organization for Standardization released a standard, ISO 22000, meant for the food industry. This standard covers the values and principles of ISO 9000 and the Hazard Analysis and Critical Control Points (HACCP) standards. It gives one single integrated standard for the food industry and is expected to become more popular in the coming years in such industry.

ISO has also released standards for other industries. For example Technical Standard (TS 16949) defines requirements in addition to those in ISO 9001:2008 specifically for the automotive industry.

ISO has a number of standards that support quality management. One group describes processes (including ISO 12207 and ISO 15288) and another describes process assessment and improvement ISO 15504.

The Software Engineering Institute has its own process assessment and improvement methods, called CMMi (Capability Maturity Model—integrated) and IDEAL respectively. These include the following:

1. TQM processes.
2. Tools and techniques.
3. People and teamwork.
4. Quality management system.
5. Performance measurement and self-assessment.

3.7.1 ISO 9000 Certification: The effects of globalization permeate every nation and society. It has brought in many changes and one of the positive outcomes is the opportunity for all business entities to participate and compete as per their individual competitive advantage with international players on a level platform. It has necessitated development of a common code for products and services to be traded: specification based on an international standard and the producers must have the capability to meet the required specification. In the circumstances, there seems to be a tacit pressure on participating companies to acquire ISO 9000 certification.

Voehl et al. (1994) note that 'ISO 9000 is a set of certification standards designed to promote international trade by creating a level playing field for producers worldwide to compete equally.' The intent is to certify individual firms as a proof of due diligence to assure customers that the firm has capability to produce quality goods and services and it follows prescribed standards and procedures. It becomes easy for a buyer to purchase goods and services from around the world and be assured of their uniform quality. ISO 9000 provides concepts and specific aspects of a quality assurance programme and ISO 9004 focuses on creating and sustaining a quality management system including human resource development issues, leadership issues and performance recognition issues. The certification process involves audits by the certifying agency which is an independent expert body and it ensures compliance for conformance to specified standards.

3.7.2 ISO 9001:2008: The ISO 9000 standard has also undergone revisions. The ISO 9000:1987 series of standards comprise ISO 9001:1987, ISO 9002:1987 and ISO 9003:1987. ISO 9001:2000 combines the three standards 9001, 9002, and 9003 into one, called 9001. The 2000 version places high priority on the concept of process management required for the monitoring the process involved and optimization of a company's tasks and activities, instead of just inspecting the final product. It also demands involvement of senior executives, in order to integrate quality into the business system and avoid delegation of quality functions to junior level. Another goal is to improve effectiveness via process performance matrix—a numerical measurement of the effectiveness of tasks and activities. Design and development procedures are required only if a company does in fact engage in the creation of new products.

ISO 9001:2008 only introduces clarifications to the existing requirements of ISO 9001:2000 and some changes intended to improve consistency with ISO 14001:2004. There are no new requirements. The requirements in ISO 9001:2008 (which is one of the standards in the ISO 9000 family) include:

1. A set of procedures that cover all key processes in the business.
2. Monitoring processes to ensure they are effective.
3. Keeping adequate records.
4. Checking output for defects, with appropriate and corrective action where necessary.
5. Regularly reviewing individual processes and the quality system itself for effectiveness.
6. Facilitating continual improvement.

3.8 Certification Process

ISO does not itself certify a business organization. Many countries have formed accreditation bodies to authorize certification bodies, which audit organizations applying for ISO 9001 compliance certification. It is commonly referred to as ISO 9000:2000 certification.

Both the accreditation bodies and the certification bodies should have received accreditation, which is a formal recognition of their competence, integrity and impartiality from the designated national authority. Almost every country has a national institution which is vested with the power for according recognition to agencies in compliance with the ISO requirement, which are as follows:

1. Principle and practice of certification in terms of the provision in ISO Handbook.
2. General requirement for the acceptance in terms of the provision contained in ISO/IEC Guide 40.

The requirement in respect of the accreditation body also

includes the following:

1. General rules of a model third party certification system for products as per ISO/IEC Guide 28.
2. Guidelines for corrective action to be taken by the certification body in the event of misuse of its mark of conformity.

The various accreditation bodies have mutual agreements with each other to ensure that certificates issued by one of these are accepted worldwide. They are at liberty to charge fees for their services on the mutually agreed terms.

The applying organization must begin the process with establishing a quality system that meets the requirements set forth by ISO 9000 which is clearly stated in the standard as checklist:

1. Management responsibility.
2. Quality system documentation.
3. Contract review.
4. Design control.
5. Purchasing.
6. Process control.
7. Inspection and testing.
8. Calibration.
9. Internal auditing.
10. Handling of rejected products.
11. Corrective action.

The list however does not describe how to meet the requirement. The responsibility lies with the individual company how it will meet each requirement. The auditors undertake a pre-assessment review, generally with the quality manager: (a) to explain the scope of assessment, assessment process, its objectives, documentation requirement, (b) to check on the statutory requirement, and (c) to highlight any obvious inadequacy which may result in denial of the certificate.

The full assessment involves a rigorous and detailed examination of quality practice and demonstrable proof that the quality policy, systems including practices are being complied with in letter and spirit. The company is assessed based on an extensive sample of its sites, functions, products, services and processes; a list of problems ("action requests" or "non-compliance") is made known to the management. If there are no major problems on this list, or after it receives a satisfactory improvement plan from the management showing how any problems will be resolved, the certification body will issue an ISO 9001 certificate for each geographical site it has visited.

A company or organization that has been independently audited and certified to be in conformance with ISO 9001 may publicly state that it is "ISO 9001 certified" or "ISO 9001 registered". It is however to be noted that certification to an ISO 9001 standard does not guarantee any quality of end products and services; rather, it certifies that formalized business processes are in place in the business entity.

An ISO certificate is not a once-and-for-all award. It is renewed at regular intervals, usually around three years, or as recommended by the certification body. There are no grades of competence within ISO 9001: either a company is certified (meaning that it is committed to the method and model of quality management described in the standard), or it is not.

3.9 Auditing/Monitoring

Organizations usually use audits to assess the financial health of a firm. It can also be applied to ascertain the outcome of any project under implementation/implemented. ASQC defines quality audit as, 'a systematic and independent examination and evaluation to determine whether quality activities and results comply with planned arrangements and whether these arrangements are implemented effectively and are suitable to achieving objectives'.

Organizations registered under ISO 9001 certification scheme may follow either of the two types of Auditing: auditing by an external agency or audits by internal staff trained for this process. The aim is continual review and assessment to verify that the system is working as it's supposed to, find out the areas where there is scope for improvement and to correct or prevent problems identified. It is considered healthier for internal auditors to audit outside their usual management line, so as to bring a degree of independence to their judgments. The certification body however undertakes unannounced surveillance audit to ensure that the system continues to work as normal and meets registration requirement. That is, the company establishes, documents, implements, and maintains a quality management system and continually improves its effectiveness in accordance with the requirements of the ISO 9001:2008.

The requirement as per ISO 9000:1994 standard was more in the nature of 'compliance auditing'. The auditors were satisfied when the written procedure was strictly followed and they used to verify the following:

1. Tell me what you do *(describe the business process).*
2. Show me where it says that *(reference the procedure manuals).*
3. Prove that this is what happened *(exhibit evidence in documented records).*

The ISO 2000 standard uses a different approach. Auditors are expected to go beyond mere 'compliance' auditing and focus on risk, status and importance. This means that they are expected to make more judgments on what is effective for the process, rather than merely adhering to what is formally prescribed. The standard practice under the 2000 version at present is more proactive; 'Will this process help you achieve your stated objectives? Is it a good process or is there a way to do it better?'

3.10 Advantages of Quality System

By now it is widely acknowledged that a business organization can improve its business with introduction of quality system with a positive return on investment, increasing market share, for the system optimally utilises the comparative advantage to achieve competitiveness. The experts believe that quality principles in ISO 9000:2000 are sound: its guidelines provide a comprehensive model for quality management systems that can make any company competitive. With ISO certification, the organization can gain many advantages, some of which are:

1. To create a more efficient, effective operation: following the standard methods and procedure for manufacture as a common practice. It establishes a quality culture in the company.
2. To attain increased business confidence.
3. To increase customer satisfaction and retention.
4. To enhance marketability of its product or services including international trade.
5. To improve employee motivation, awareness, and morale.
6. To increase profitability consequent to reduction of waste and increase in productivity.

The intangible gains like increased business confidence, brand name, good will are added advantage.

Research studies confirm the efficacy of ISO 9000 certification system; for example, the benefits at DuPont plant over a span of about a year were overwhelming. Hockman [2] elaborates the major gains:

1. On-time delivery at one plant increased from 70 percent to 90 percent.
2. Cycle time decreased from 15 days to 1.5 days.
3. The number of errors at one warehouse decreased by 95 percent.
4. The number of necessary test procedures at one site decreased from 3,000 to 1,100.

3.11 Effectiveness of ISO Certification

For ISO certification to be an effective system in a company, its proper implementation and practice in accordance with the requirements of the standard are crucial.

Some of the important aspects are discussed below:

1. Commitment of Senior Management for improving the quality of product and services and taking steps necessary is essential, lest the certificate remains a decoration on the wall. Top management must be committed to the development and implementation of the quality management system. The effectiveness of the organization improves by:
   - Ensuring the availability of required resources.
   - Establishing a quality policy.
   - Ensuring that quality objectives are defined.
   - Creating a good working environment that nurtures total commitment of all employees.
   - Conducting management reviews, taking corrective action as per monitoring report.
   - Communicating with suppliers, employees and customer about the company's vision, policy and sincere efforts to meet customers' needs and preferences.
2. The ISO system should be integrated into the business practices. It is often noticed that many organizations get ISO certification but continue with existing practices. The system initiated should not remain confined to the documentation.
3. The system should focus on continuous improvement based on the customer experience—incorporating 'voice of the customer' in the product through design to marketing including after sales service in order to exceed customer expectation.
4. The findings of the auditor need to be taken seriously and implemented in areas where improvement is necessary. There are instances that management doesn't understand the business implications and simply ignore the reports. This is not in the interest of the organization. Japanese industry considers finding shortcomings an opportunity. It takes full advantage of it to identify the root cause for

rectification. This offers tremendous potential to emulate.

It is relevant to note the remarks of a quality consultant, 'Good business judgment is needed to determine its proper role for a company. Is certification itself important to the marketing plans of the company? If not, do not rush to certification. Even without certification, companies should utilize the ISO 9000 model as a benchmark to assess the adequacy of its quality programs.'

End Notes

1. International Organization for Standardization is a worldwide federation of national standard bodies.
2. Hockman, K.K. '*Taking Mystery Out of Quality*' Training and Development, July 1992: 36.

4

Tools and Techniques of Quality

Over the years, many thinkers and experts have enriched the quality management system with meaningful contribution. A wide range of concepts, tools, techniques, methods and approaches that have evolved after long trials and refinements are included in the quality literature. The industry has greatly benefited from the application of these tools, techniques and approaches. A detailed presentation of the development of quality concepts is in chapter 2 and an elaboration of the quality tools and techniques follows.

4.1 Seven Basic Tools of Quality

The quality tools are intellectual application of scientific principles and methods for improving physical processes and systems in business and industry in order to get quality output. The application of the tools in practice is basically for the identification of causes of the process variation and to offer probable solutions that would result in improvement of process for quality output that meets the customers' expectations. While most of these tools find universal application in quality management practices, a few are suitable for specific situation for desired result.

The seven basic tools of quality is a designation given to a set of statistical and graphical methods identified as being most useful for troubleshooting the problems that influence quality of product. Post-War, Japanese companies that had set about training their workforces in statistical quality control found that the complexity of the subject intimidated the vast majority of their workers and scaled back training to focus primarily on simpler methods that would suffice to deal with most quality-related issues. Inspired by the outcome on application these seven basic and simple approaches, the designation gained popularity. The seven basic tools stand in contrast to the more advanced statistical methods developed in the field of operations research. They are termed as basic because persons with a basic training in statistics can use these tools to solve a vast majority of quality-related problems. It is mentioned that the advanced techniques and approaches like JIT, SPC, Six Sigma are more than just tools and therefore separately presented.

The seven basic tools of quality are as under:

1. Fishbone Diagram.
2. Check Sheet.
3. Run Charts and Control Charts.
4. Histogram.
5. Pareto Chart.
6. Scatter Diagram.
7. Stratification.

4.1.1 Fishbone Diagram (Cause-and-Effect Diagram)

The quality movement pioneered by Kaoru Ishikawa in Japan began in Kawasaki shipyards. He attempted application of new approaches and methods for managing quality and became one of the distinguished quality experts on quality management in industry. The cause-and-effect diagram (C&E diagram) is one of his profound contributions in the development of quality tools. It is one of the seven basic tools which are not based on statistical principles.

The C&E diagram is also known as the fishbone diagram because its presentation resembles the skeleton of a fish, with the main causal categories drawn as 'bones' attached to the spine of the fish. The concept is used to explore all the potential or real causes (or inputs) that result in a single effect (or output). The ribs represent probable causes that may lead to the effect. The ribs are assigned to the major factors (five Ms: man, machine, material, money and method) and lower level factors as branches of the rib. Causes are arranged according to their level of importance, resulting in a depiction of relationships and hierarchy of events. This helps in the search for root causes, identifying areas where there may be problems in comparison with the relative importance of different causes.

To begin with the team comprising of operators, supervisors having direct working experience on manufacture develops a list of possible factors in a brainstorming session. The ideas generated are noted systematically and the diagram is constructed. It reveals the interrelationship which otherwise would not be so obvious. The presentation also clearly points out the factors that influence the process which are to be taken care of. It serves as an excellent reminder to the operators what needs their attention most.

The diagram (Figure 4.1) presented below shows how various factors associated in the process affect output.

Figure 4.1: Fishbone Diagram

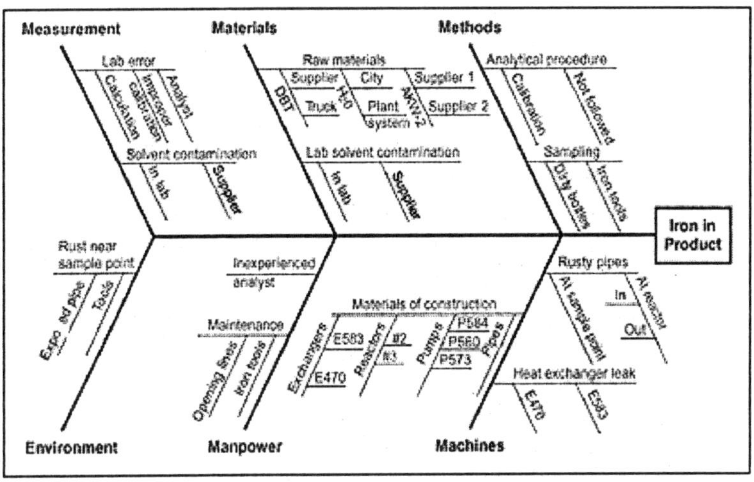

Source: Tague, Nancy R. '*The Quality Toolbox*' ASQ Quality Press, 2004:247-249).

Theoretically, the causes should be arranged into four

major categories, viz.

1. Manpower, methods, materials, and machinery (recommended for manufacturing).
2. Equipment, policies, procedures, and people (recommended for administration and service).

In practice however these should serve as helpful guidelines and need not be binding in case they limit the diagram or are considered inappropriate. For example, the diagram above depicts causes in six major categories. It is an analysis for understanding the source of periodic iron contamination problem by a manufacturing team. The six generic headings prompt ideas. Layers of branches show thorough thinking about the causes of the problem: under the heading 'machines', the idea 'materials of construction' shows four kinds of equipment and then several specific machine numbers. It may also be noted that some ideas appear in two different places. 'Calibration' shows up under 'methods' as a factor in the analytical procedure, and also under 'measurement' as a cause of lab error. 'Iron tools' can be considered a 'methods' problem when taking samples or a 'manpower' problem with maintenance personnel.

It is typically useful for identifying the cause of imperfection in the process for finding the right solution. Ishikawa in '*Guide to Quality Control*' explains the benefits of applying fishbone diagram in decision making process as given below:

1. Developing the diagram itself is an enlightening and instructive process.
2. Such diagram focuses the group and thus preventing irrelevant discussion.
3. It separates causes from symptoms.

4.1.2 Check Sheet: Check sheet has proved to be a valuable tool in a variety of application for identification of problems. On a factory floor many operators work with a number of machines and the production data is available. A simple document is designed for collecting data in real-time. It is placed at the location where the data is generated for easy noting and display. The document is a typical blank form that is meant for quick, easy, and efficient recording of the desired information, which can be either quantitative or qualitative. [1] When the information is quantitative, the check sheet is sometimes called a tally sheet.

A defining characteristic of a check sheet is that data is recorded by making marks ('checks') on it. Usually these check sheets will have a list of the defects or problems that may occur in the process. When a sample is taken and inspected, a mark is placed in the appropriate column in case a defect or a problem has been noted. Taking measurement of the sample and logging the data on the check sheet should ideally be done by the operator who runs the machine and not the quality control inspector. [2] The number of marks on the sheet and their distribution pattern reveal the area of weakness and cause of developing defects and/or poor efficiency. The check sheets are of five basic types:

1. Classification: for classifying a defect or failure mode into specific categories.
2. Location: the physical location of a defect in respect of a part or item being evaluated is indicated on a sheet.
3. Frequency: the presence of a defect or combination of defects in respect of a part is indicated and the occurrences are analyzed.
4. Measurement Scale: a measurement scale is divided into intervals, and measurements are indicated by checking an appropriate interval.
5. Check List: the items to be performed for a task are listed so that, as each is accomplished, it can be indicated as having been completed.

The check sheet is then analyzed to identify what types of problems or defects are occurring in the process and the reasons there of. The type of data used in the defective item check sheets is countable data. Consider for example, a factory producing a component. The critical specification of the part is to be noted on the 'process distribution check sheet'. The data can be collected for a week and analyzed for locating the problem that generates defective parts. The analysis can be in respect of machines, or operators, or for defect type in the production process. The relative performance evidences where the fault lies and action required to solve them for improving the process. A typical Defect Location Check Sheet is shown in Table 4.1 which has been prepared based on the defects noted from samples and logged. The data relates to defects generated in the process of manufacturing a component by the wave solder process.

Table 4.1: Defect Type Check Sheet

Defect type	Insufficient solder	Cold solder	Solder bridge	Excess solder	Blow holes
Frequency	//// //	//	///	///	//// //// ////
Total	7	2	3	2	14

The above example relates to one variable (particular defect). The data evinces that 'blow holes' and 'insufficient solder' require technical analysis and process rectification to eliminate major defects.

The matrix below (Table 4.2) presents a frequency tabulation of two variables—data in respect of operators (A to F) and error types (1 to 6).

According to Pareto Principle, operator B and E and error type 3 and 5 need immediate attention. Analysis of B's performance would reveal that his performance with respect to error type 3 may be due to his misinterpretation of instruction, inadequate training or lack of clarity on procedure. The performance of E is poor with regard to all error types is a cause of concern: either he is not fit for the job, he has not been properly trained or his wilful delinquency. It needs examination for remedial action.

Table 4.2: Performance Check sheet

Error type	Operators						Total
	A	B	C	D	E	F	
1			1		2		3
2	1				1		2
3		16	1		2		19
4					1		1
5	2	1	3	1	4	2	13
6					3		3
Total	3	17	5	1	13	2	41

4.1.3 Run Charts and Control Charts:

The run charts and control chart are one type of the seven basic tools of quality control. Shewhart and Deming are credited with the development and applications of the control chart for analyzing the processes for attaining continuous improvement in industry. These charts can be seen as part of an objective and disciplined approach that enables correct decisions regarding control of the process, including whether or not to change process control parameters. Process parameters should never be adjusted for a process that is in control, as this will result in degraded process performance.

A. Run Charts: A Run chart is prepared by plotting the sampling inspection data over a specified period of time: x-axis time and y-axis output (result of performance). It is used to scientifically track performance trend of individual worker, each machine, including the trend in defects generated. The declining trend in performance naturally attracts the attention of the management for action and any trend indicating better output offers why and how it has happened for others to follow. The best performance gives new target that is achievable.

The run chart is strikingly simple but its limitations, in fact, are that it does not help to indicate whether the process variable is due to assignable cause that could be rectified and whether the process is capable of production as per the specification desired (process capability). A control chart has been designed to take care of these shortcomings.

B. Control Charts: A control chart offers a very specific advantage: it allows differentiating significant changes from the natural variability of the process. With the basic knowledge of statistics, one can calculate the mean, range, standard deviation, percent defective and fraction defect from the sampling inspection data. The control limits are also calculated and control charts are developed. Its analysis is to get definite information about the process: whether the process is currently under control, or the variations noted are wide calling the attention of the operator for rectification. When the variations are within the control limits, it indicates that it is stable and that the marginal deviations are coming from sources inherent to the process. This data from the process can also be used to predict the future performance of the process. And in case the chart indicates that the process being monitored is not in control-deviations are beyond the control limits, it calls for determining the sources of variation to be eliminated immediately to bring the process back into control.

The control chart (Figure 4.2) shows a practical data recorded as per inspection result.

Figure 4.2: Control Chart

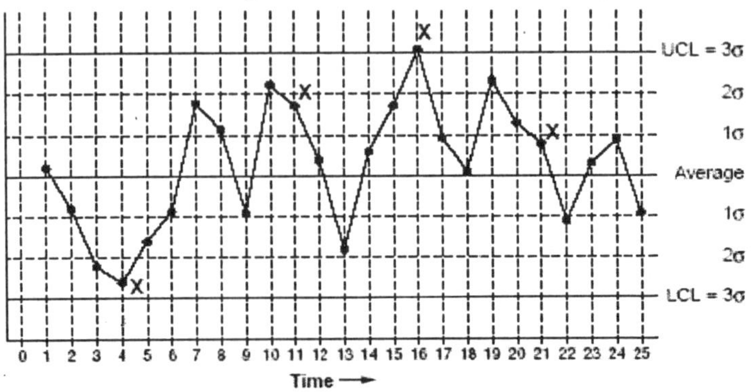

Source: Tague, Nancy R. '*The Quality Toolbox*' ASQ Quality Press, 2004: 155-158.

The information is also interpreted for suitable action. Out-of-control signals that should attract attention for corrective action are as follows:

1. A single point outside the control limits—point 16 is above the upper control limit.
2. Two out of three successive points are on the same side of the centreline and farther than 2σ from it— point 4 sends this signal.
3. Four out of five successive points are on the same side of the centreline and farther than 1σ from it—point 11 indicates this situation.
4. A run of eight, that is, eight observations in a row are on the same side of the centreline—point 21 is eighth in a row above the centreline. 10 out of 11, 12 out of 14 or 16 out of 20 on the same side of the centreline in a row also signal out-of-control situation.
5. Obvious consistent or persistent patterns that suggest something unusual about the process.

Thus control charts reveal the process imperfection which otherwise could not have been noticed by the operator or supervisor. It is therefore deployed as a basic tool for continuous improvement. As the process is refined and improved, the UCL and LCL can also be modified. The measurement and plotting being instantaneous, there is no delay in detection and taking corrective action as and when required. It is on real time basis.

4.1.4 Histogram: Histogram is a graphical representation, showing a visual impression of the distribution of experimental data. It represents a frequency distribution by means of rectangles whose widths represent class intervals and whose areas are proportional to the corresponding frequencies. The intervals are placed together in order to show that the data represented by the histogram, while exclusive, is also continuous.

The term is derived from 'histos 'anything set upright and 'gramma 'drawing, recording, writing' and Karl Pearson who introduced the term in 1895 mentioned to have derived the name from 'historical diagram'. The presentation of data as a summary conveys the following important information:

1. The general shape of the frequency distribution (normal, chi-square, etc.).
2. Symmetry of the distribution—even or skewed.
3. Modality—uni-modal, bi-modal, or multi-modal.
4. The probability distribution of the data.

A histogram is used to chart frequency of occurrence. Suppose there exist a great deal of variation in a process of manufacture and the management is interested to decide a standard time for the manufacture, the immediate temptation is to compute the average. This is not realistic. The most frequent time is more appropriate standard which is revealed by a histogram.

Process variability can be calculated from the data by histogram: flatter and wider the frequency distribution, the greater the process variability. The visual presentation is a helpful means of measuring, understanding and discussing the variability which is natural to all processes due to a number of factors. In order to understand the important facts and interpretation of the chart, some basic knowledge of statistics, like variable and attribute data, measures of central tendency-mean, standard deviation are necessary.

In cases the distribution is known, a histogram that does not fit the distribution may provide clues about a process and measurement problem. For example, a histogram that shows a higher than normal frequency in bins near one end and then a sharp drop-off may indicate that the observer is 'helping' the results by classifying extreme data in the less extreme group.

4.1.5 Pareto Chart: Pareto chart is a very useful tool not only in manufacturing but where ever there is need for separating the vital from trivial with statistical display chart. It is considered one of the basic tools in management practice in addition to being one of the seven basic tools of quality management. The chart is named after its creator, Italian economist Vilfredo Pareto (1848-1923). With his insight, he realized that in real world only a few causes have major effects and there are many causes with limited consequence. Thus, it is worthwhile to concentrate on the few: for example, as it has been proved in practice, 20 percent of problems associated with a process usually produce 80 percent of product defects or 80 percent of the cost arise from 20 percent of the defect types. [3]

The purpose of the Pareto chart is to highlight the most important among a typically large set of factors. In quality control it often represents the most common sources of defects, the highest occurring type of defect, or the most frequent reasons for customer complaints, and so on.

It is a type of chart that contains both bar and line graph, where individual values are represented in descending order by bars, and the cumulative total is represented by the line.

Consider some practical application, such as a company marketing products in different regions or for different age-groups may prepare a Pareto Chart for region-wise or age-group wise percent of sales over a period. It will clearly show that more than 80 percent of sales are in two or three regions and in respect of a few age groups enabling the management to decide future course of action. Similarly, Pareto chart in respect of failures and re-work of an equipment shows that more than three-fourth of the failure rates has been due to only one or two components that require immediate attention for redesign for production or alternate sourcing.

4.1.6 Scatter Diagram: Scatter diagrams are used to graphically represent the relationship between two variables and it is used when a variable exists that is under the control of the experimenter. If a parameter exists that is systematically incremented and/or decremented by the other, it is called the control parameter or independent variable and is customarily plotted along the horizontal axis. The measured or dependent variable is customarily plotted along the vertical axis. If no dependent variable exists, either type of variable can be plotted on both axis, and a scatter plot will illustrate only the degree of correlation (not causation) between two variables.

A scatter plot can suggest various kinds of correlations between variables with a certain confidence level. Correlations may be positive (rising), negative (falling), or null (uncorrelated). If the pattern of dots slopes from lower left to upper right, it suggests a positive correlation between the variables being studied. If the pattern of dots slopes from upper left to lower right, it suggests a negative correlation. A line of best fit (alternatively called 'trendline') can be drawn in order to study the correlation between the variables. An equation for the correlation between the variables can be determined by established best-fit procedures. For a linear correlation, the best-fit procedure is known as linear regression and is guaranteed to generate a correct solution in a finite time. Unfortunately, no universal best-fit procedure is guaranteed to generate a correct solution for arbitrary relationships.

One of the most powerful aspects of a scatter plot, however, is its ability to show nonlinear relationships between variables. Furthermore, if the data is represented by a mixture model of simple relationships, these relationships will be visually evident as superimposed patterns.

Consider, for example a practical application in industry: a company wants to find how effective is the training programme of operators and what the optimal duration is, a scatter diagram can be plotted between training (by hours/days) and the defect rate. Similarly, the correlation between speed of an automobile and fuel consumption, surface finish and machine speed can be plotted. It is also possible to determine correlation between two process factors-cleaning time and temperature of the cleaning solution. With this information, the cycle time can be reduced logically, for reduced cycle time increases profit as a result of cost reduction.

4.1.7 Stratification: Stratification is the process of grouping members of the population into relatively homogeneous subgroups before sampling. The strata should be mutually exclusive: every element in the population must be assigned to only one stratum. The strata should also be collectively exhaustive: no population element can be excluded. And in case the population density varies greatly within a region, stratified sampling will ensure that estimates can be made with equal accuracy in different parts of the region, and that comparisons of sub-regions can be made with equal clarity and correctness.

Stratification also involves grouping of data into categories such as relating to operators, machines or specific material. The group data collected over a period is graphically presented and analyzed for finding clues that would help better performance. For example, consider a factory where five assembly line operators work independently for the same product output. The group data along with data in respect of each operator is stratified-plotted for the group and operator-wise. The graph clearly provides the relative performance of five operators and the group average. The data can be output (performance) or operator induced defect generated during the period or both plotted separately.

The relative performance indicates which operator has achieved best performance, minimum defect and which are below average performance and above average defects. This calls for management attention:

1. To identify causes why the performance of some are poor for suitable remedial action.
2. What makes some better performers—for others to learn?

In a sense, Pareto chart is also a stratified data analysis for revealing the cause for decision making. These are powerful tools used for continuous improvement of process, people leading to better performance.

4.2 Other Quality Tools

The seven tools described above are referred to by Ishikawa as 'the seven indispensable tools for quality control'.

These represent the basic methods most useful at work place for solving quality problems. There are however other tools which have been developed during the course of various applications and now added to the list. These include Flow Chart, the Survey and Design of experiment are important among others.

4.2.1 Flow Chart: A flow chart, as the name suggests, relates to charting the flow of a process from inputs to output indicating the operation step by step indicating the types of function involved. It gives a clear picture where each operator fits in, his responsibility and how his contribution influences the entire process. This understanding of the process is necessary for solving any problem or improving the process. More often than not, people who are working directly with a process are amazed to find out how little they understand the complete process and how evident it is with the flow diagram.

A flow chart also suggests if there is any requirement of application other tool and technique for analysis.

4.2.2 The Survey: A survey is finding information on a relevant subject, for example how the internal customer and external customers rate the company's product or service. A structured and well thought of questionnaire with direct questions soliciting specific answers usually prove very useful. It is however necessary that the questions should be simple, unambiguous to elicit response that is factual, spontaneous and unbiased.

4.2.3 Design of Experiment: Design of experiment (DOX) is a very sophisticated method for experimenting complex processes with the objective of optimizing it. When a number of variables influence the process, experiment can be designed for controlling important variable and ascertaining criteria for optimization. DOX also shows which of the factors are critical for the process enabling the quality personnel to apply control for those parameters.

4.3 Techniques and Approaches

The techniques and approaches that evolved under the

broader concept of total quality system help to analyze problems relating to quality in industry and find solution. Some important techniques and their application are discussed below.

4.3.1 Statistical Quality Control: Statistical Quality Control (SQC) is a technique for controlling quality of product using a set of statistical tools. Walter A. Shewhart, a distinguished quality professional developed this approach employing the concepts of statistics [4] for evaluation of quality of products and processes. Deming applied the technique for quality control in industry in the United States during World War specifically for improving quality in the manufacture of munitions and other strategically important products. Dodge (1925) introduced the basic concept of sampling inspection followed by L.H.C. Tippett in 1935.

The concept has since been developed further, refined and used in almost all the manufacturing sectors for various applications. SQC rules broadly comprise three important elements:

1. One, descriptive statistics—statistical methods that summarize or describe collection of data is descriptive statistics. It is the measure of central tendency and dispersion of the data which in statistics referred to as the mean, standard deviation, the range. These are used to describe basic quality characteristics such as the central tendency and variability of observed data and their relationships.
2. Two, acceptance sampling—the process involves randomly taking sample from a production process for inspection and deciding directly whether desirable quality has been achieved in respect of the batch of products and accept or reject the entire lot based on the results. It has been a common quality control technique used in industry and particularly the military in contracts for procurement. During World War, the practice became common and industry still uses the approach for quality checks on

procured items used as inputs in the production process.

3. Three, the statistical process control (SPC) that involves inspection of random samples picked up from the output of a process and deciding whether the product characteristics are within a predetermined range. The result indicates whether the process is functioning properly or it requires analysis and rectification for quality output.

All three of these are integrated to form the foundation of statistical quality control. It is helpful for measurement and evaluation of the quality of products or services. The analysis using this technique provides different types of information for improving the process. While the descriptive statistics provide certain basic inputs which are helpful, they are inadequate to analyze problems in relation to the quality of output. The acceptance sampling is useful in acceptance decision, but the information collected relates to the product after it has been manufactured. It does not help to identify the quality problem during the production process for taking remedial action so that wastages are eliminated. The statistical process control (SPC) technique however provides insight to the production process and in case there is problem, the causes are identified for corrective action and thus eliminating the cause in order that defective output is not further generated in the manufacturing process.

A quality defect means deviation from the predetermined specification. It is primarily due to variation in the production process resulting in lack of product consistency. The control chart is an important device to find out the nature of variation in a process: natural/random variation or a variation due to an assignable cause. The assignable causes of variation can be precisely identified and eliminated using this technique. Examples of this type of variation are due to poor quality of raw materials, an operator's performance-may be he needs more training, or due to a machine in need of repair. In each of these cases the problem can be identified and corrected and quality of the output is assured, by restoring the production process into the state of control.

4.3.2 Control Charts: The most commonly used tool for monitoring the product quality is a control chart. A control chart is a graphic representation of variation with mean as the centre line and permissible tolerance as upper control limit and lower control limit. It is designed to monitor specific defect type: the critical parameters measured follow continuous variable probability distribution-'Normal distribution' pattern, or discrete distribution—'Binomial distribution' with two possible outcome, e.g. success or failure and 'Poison distribution' applied in respect of defects per metre of cloth and number of pinholes in a glass bottle. The inspection data plotted on the chart clearly shows the nature of variation which is interpreted by the operator for remedial action, if any.

4.3.3 Control Limits and Risks: The limits of variation gives the control chart analytical power and enables the user to instantly detect whether the production process is out of control. The control limits being +3 σ (standard deviation) from the mean are dependent on the sample size; larger the sample size, smaller the standard deviation and closer the control limit. Therefore, in case of varying sample size control limits are decided on the basis of average sample size. Another procedure is to change the scale for standard deviation to take care of the variation in sample size.

Depending on the process parameter, the control charts are designed; such as variable—a measurable quantity (diameter of a shaft), or attribute—number of defectives in a sample and number of defects per unit.

4.3.4 Control Chart for Variables: A control chart based on the measurement of quality characteristics is called control chart for variables. It is used to monitor characteristics that can be measured and have a continuum of values, such as height, weight, or volume. A soft drink bottling operation is an example of a variable measure, since the amount of liquid in the bottles is measured and can take on a number of different values. Other examples are the weight of a bag of sugar, the temperature in a baking oven, or the diameter of a metal pipe.

4.3.5 X-bar Chart: A mean control chart is often referred to as an x-bar chart. It is used to monitor changes in the mean that is the desired specification. To construct a mean chart, the centre line of the chart is the computed mean of the multiple samples. Usually these sample sizes are small, about four or five observations.

The upper and lower control limits on a control chart are usually set at +3 standard deviations (σ) from the mean. It is assumed that the data exhibit a normal distribution and the control limits will capture 99.74 percent of the normal variation. Control limits can be set at +2 σ from the mean. In that case, control limits would capture 95.44 percent of the values.

4.3.6 Range (R) Chart: Range (R) charts are another type of control chart for variables, the centre line is R-bar, computed from a set of multiple samples, where R denotes the range (difference between the maximum and minimum value in each sample) and R-bar is the mean value of Rs. It is widely used n industry for measuring dispersion of the important quality characteristics. The control limits are:

X-R Chart:

Upper control limit (UCL) = $\bar{\bar{X}} + A_2\bar{R}$

Lower control limit (LCL) = $\bar{\bar{X}} - A_2\bar{R}$

R-Chart:

Upper control limit (UCL) = $D_4\,\bar{R}$

Lower control limit (LCL) = $D_3\bar{R}$

The values of the constants A_2, D_3, D_4 are dependent on the sample size and readily available from standard table in quality handbook. Table 4.3 shows some representative data borrowed from standard tables.

4.3.7 Control Chart for Attributes: A control chart for attributes, on the other hand, is used to monitor characteristics that follow discrete distribution, often can be evaluated with a simple yes or no decision. The most common types of control charts for attributes are p-charts and c-charts.

Table 4.3: Constants for Control Charts

N	A_2	D_3	D_4
2	1.880	0	3.267
3	1.023	0	2.575
4	0.729	0	2.282
5	0.577	0	2.115

4.3.8 P-Chart: P-charts are used to measure the proportion of items in a sample that are defective. Examples are the proportion of broken cookies in a batch/box. P-charts are appropriate when both the number of defectives measured and the size of the total sample can be counted. A proportion can then be computed and used as the statistic of measurement.

Upper control limit (UCL) = $\bar{p} + z\sigma_p$

Lower control limit (LCL) = $\bar{p} - z\sigma_p$

4.3.9 C-Chart: C-charts are used to monitor the number of defects per unit. The actual number of defects in a sample are counted and plotted. For example, we can count the number of complaints from customers in a month, the number of bacteria on a Petri dish, or the number of barnacles on the bottom of a boat.

Upper control limit (UCL) = $\bar{c} + Z\sqrt{\bar{c}}$

Lower control limit (LCL) = $\bar{c} - Z\sqrt{\bar{c}}$

4.3.10 Operating Characteristic Curve: The Operating Characteristic (OC) Curve shows how sensitive the control chart is for the detection of changes in process parameter. A control chart, especially the control limits thus has to be designed with a realistic value and the uniqueness of the process. When control limits are tighter, its effect is to pull the OC curve and reduce the risk of not detecting a shift in the process. [5]

4.4 Statistical Process Control (SPC)

Statistical Process Control (SPC) is the application of theory of statistics in monitoring and control of a process to ensure that it operates at its full potential to produce conforming product. Dr. Walter Shewhart deserves credit for the origin of the statistical process control (SPC) concept. While working at Bell Laboratories, he realized that the data generated from the normal practice of quality control during the process of manufacture could be used to determine whether the process is in control or being affected by special causes that need attention for rectification for quality output. The statistical quality control charts that Shewhart developed paved the way for a quality revolution which is now called 'total quality'. [6]

4.4.1 What is SPC? SPC is a statistical method of separating variation resulting from special causes and the natural variation in order to eliminate the special causes and establish and maintain consistency in the process, enabling process improved (Goetsch and Davis, 1994:488). Production in a factory is a process, which may be affected by multiple factors. Variation being the enemy of quality, the technique, SPC can be applied to control the variation in production process for elimination or substantial reduction of waste and achieving continuous improvement.

As explained earlier, variation results from two kinds of causes: assignable cause and natural or random causes. SPC utilizes the control chart as a tool for eliminating all controllable causes responsible for variation in the process. The workers are in a position to detect assignable causes of variation from the natural causes and analyze the special causes associated with five Ms: man, machine, material, method and measurement to identify for remedy. [7] Once the root cause is rectified, the process is said to be in statistical control. At this stable state, 99.74 percent of output should be within statistical control limits. The technique thus helps to improve quality of output of the manufacturing process resulting in cost reduction.

In the context of understanding how SPC comes into play in key aspects like control of variation, elimination of waste, predictability of process and benefits there of, these are discussed below.

4.4.2 Process Capability: Process Capability means the ability of a production process to meet or exceed preset specifications. And in order to understand exactly what this means, let's look more closely at the term specification. The design engineer decides the specifications with tolerance limits and mentions in the drawing of the dimension of parts/components. The product dimension is acceptable quality characteristic for all concerned: the operator's duty is to manufacture items within this preset range and the quality personnel to check for conformance. Otherwise, the product is not acceptable.

For example, the specifications for the diameter of a machine part may be specified as 15 + .03 cm. This means that the diameter of the part should be 15 cm, though it is acceptable if it falls within the limits of 14.97 cm and 15.03 cm. Similarly a bottle of perfume should be filled with 16 ml of liquid, with tolerance + .02 would mean that the volume could be as low as 15.98 or as high as 16.02 ml.

The process capability analysis aims at ensuring that machine used for manufacture of the machine part or filling a bottle of perfume is capable to produce or fill within the specification limits respectively. The output of a process can be plotted in a graph; x-axis representing measurement of a parameter and y-axis the frequency counts of the measurement of the product. With no special causes affecting the process, that is operating properly, the frequency distribution curve would be a normal curve and as per its property, 99.74 percent of the process output will be within +3 standard deviations (σ) about the mean. [8] The variation about the mean is the result of natural causes. The process remains stable and output consistent so long it is free from special causes.

The result of this sample can be utilized to understand the capability of a manufacturing process and while allocating the process for the job to be done; this parameter is the deciding criteria—the tolerance requirement and the process variation should match.

It is measured by the process capability index, Cp, which is computed as the ratio of the specification width to the width of the process variability and there are three possible ranges of values for Cp that are interpreted:

1. **When, Cp=1:** Value of Cp equal to 1 means that the process variability just meets specifications that is the process is minimally capable.
2. **When, Cp<1:** Value of Cp below 1 means that the process variability is outside the range of specification, that is the process is not capable of producing within specification and the process must be improved.
3. **When, Cp>1:** Value of Cp above 1 means that the process variability is tighter than specifications and the process exceeds minimal capability.

It has one limitation: it assumes that process variability is centred on the specification range. This is however not always the case. In case the mean shifts in the process, the analysis will not reflect the true process capability.

4.4.3 Control of Variation: When any assignable causes are introduced in the process, the resulting data from inspection plotted on the control chart appears outside the control limits. It confirms that the output is defective and the process needs immediate attention for elimination of the causes. Some of the quality tools are used, for example a flow diagram to properly understand the process and a fishbone diagram for identifying the special causes of variation. The process is then rectified and the variations are controlled.

4.4.4 Benefits:

1. In most cases, waste is generated when the process is out of control-process is adversely affected by the special causes of variation. The special causes are eliminated; the process becomes stable with desired quality output. The product gains competitive advantage. SPC is a very powerful technique to be applied for waste reduction to the minimum.
2. In addition to reducing waste, SPC can lead to reduction in the time required to produce a product or service from beginning to end. As a result, there is a diminished likelihood that the final product will have to be reworked. The SPC data may also be used to identify bottlenecks, wait times, and other sources of delays within the process. Process cycle time reductions coupled with improvements in yield have made SPC a valuable tool from both; cost reduction and a customer satisfaction standpoint.
3. When the process is in the state of statistical control, its trend is monitored using control charts continuously. It is to be noted that SPC demands continuous monitoring of the process output enabling the operators to take immediate action for remedy.

4.5 Roadmap for Implementation

Quality experts suggest different procedure for implementations of the SPC concept for each firm, for every process is unique and requires specific application of the technique. As it involves technicalities, support of an expert consultant has merit. Important steps for implementation are divided into three phases: preparation, planning and execution.

4.5.1 Preparation Phase: It comprises the following three steps:

1. Commitment for providing resources–money, time,

personnel and of course the will to sincere implementation.

2. Selection of a team for implementation from concerned department—marketing, design, manufacture and quality.
3. Basic training to the team members by experts from within or by a consultant.

4.5.2 Planning Phase: When the team understands the process and identifies the process to be monitored for control and set well defined objectives, the management should take care of the following:

1. Training of operators, supervisor along with personnel from quality department who support them. The training should be specifically designed for better understanding the process and application quality tools.
2. Preparing flow chart for the process to reveal the process features and the way it actually works. It helps to identify where and why the faults occur.
3. Delegating responsibility to the operators and provide required measuring tools.

4.5.3 Execution Phase: This phase is crucial to success of the implementation. The steps involve are as follows:

1. Developing control chart and designing inspection plan.
2. Collecting sample for inspection, analyzing the trend to eliminate special causes of variation.
3. Determining process capability and continue with continuous improvement by narrowing the limits.

With its emphasis on early detection and prevention of problems, SPC has a distinct advantage over other quality methods, such as quality control by inspection which involves mainly separating defectives after they have been produced. SPC can also be usefully applied to non-manufacturing processes, such as software engineering processes, in the Capability Maturity Model Integration (CMMI). The application of SPC is a useful tool to non-repetitive, knowledge-intensive processes such as engineering processes, though it has encountered much scepticism and remains controversial today.

4.6 Inspection Planning

The critical link between design, manufacturing and quality control cannot be overstated. While for decades, dimensional measurement has served as the foundation for the inspection for controlling quality with the required set up that validates and maintains manufacturing integrity, these days, enlightened quality control focuses not on products coming off the production line but on the manufacturing process as a whole in order to ensure each operation functions optimally.

Quality management practice aims at integrating the inspection data with the manufacturing process to provide close to real-time knowledge of production and process health as well as guidance for process control and improvement. It not only reduces waste to the minimum and optimizes equipment use, personnel and material, but also puts responsibility for quality into the hands of the people who make the product. The quality management function therefore necessitates planning for measurement properly and adequately to know exactly the status of the manufacturing process and the need for improvement. It involves inspection planning.

An inspection in generic sense connotes an organized examination or formal evaluation exercise. It encompasses proper measurement and test with instruments including visual observation applied to certain characteristics of an object or activity. The results are usually compared with specified requirements and standards for determining whether the item or activity is in line with the targets. The role of inspection is to verify and validate the variance data and strictly, it does not involve separating the good from the bad as it used to be applicable in quality control procedure.

An inspection plan defines systematically the measurement to be taken, instruments to be used and the periodicity of measurement translating the design intent into a set of inspection instructions—often a marked-up blueprint with hand-drawn annotations indicating the datum to use, features to inspect and tolerances to comply with. Inspecting a work piece with reference to its dimension and other specified characteristics is to ensure conformity to design criteria and is an integral part of manufacturing. Inspections are usually non-destructive.

The objective of inspection is different as per use, for example, inspection of items received, inspection of products during the process of manufacture, inspection of final product and inspection for carrying out an audit.

4.6.1 Incoming Inspection: A company generally procures a number of items, viz. raw materials, components, consumables and the supplies received are inspected for quality conformance. This is termed as incoming inspection. It embraces checking of initial sample and lots of goods received for acceptance. The purpose of initial sample is to provide the vendee to assess the quality of the vendor's product, as representative of future supply. The vendor gets feedback on the quality level of the product and undertakes improvement, if required.

The primary reason for incoming inspection of the lot is to prevent entry of materials and components that do not satisfy quality standard specified in the production process and consequently giving rise to waste. With growing trend towards small inventories, inputs are received in weekly or a few days basis for production. Any defective lot therefore is likely to create serious problems in production schedule. The company thus has to make proper vendor selection, vendor rating, provide them detailed requirement and feedback in order to maintain high degree of uniformity in their deliveries. The procedure adopted in practice is acceptance sampling.

4.6.2 Acceptance Sampling: Acceptance sampling is a well accepted practice of checking quality of incoming lot delivered by a vendor. The process, initially applied for military procurement during the World War continues to be in practice. It involves randomly inspecting a sample from the lot and deciding whether to accept the entire lot based on the basis of the inspection. Single sampling plan, double sampling plan, multiple sampling plan are in vogue. The system is well documented in ISO 2859. [9]

4.6.3 Single Sampling Plan: Single sampling is used for inspecting the incoming lot for quality conformance. The process involves taking a random sample of size 'n', checking each unit of the sample with respect to its critical parameters as per specification. If defects found in the sample is less than or equal to the stated number 'c', the lot is accepted and in case the defects are greater than 'c' it is rejected. [10] A schematic presentation is presented in Figure 4.3.

Figure 4.3: Single Sampling Plan

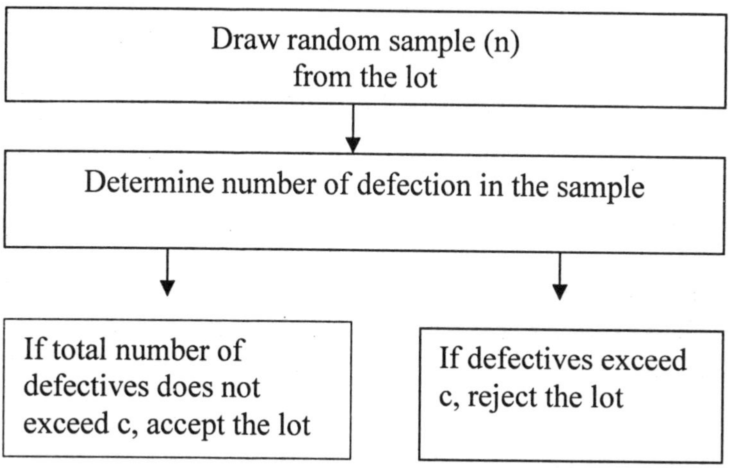

4.6.4 Double Sampling Plan: In this plan, a random first sample of size 'n_1' is drawn from the lot of material received and tested as per specification. The lot is accepted, if the number of defects does not exceed 'c_1' and reject if the number of defects equals or exceeds 'r_1'. And in case, defectives exceed c_1 but less than r_1, draw second sample 'n_2' and decide acceptance or rejection as per the schematic diagram (Figure 4.4).

Figure 4.4: Double Sampling Plan

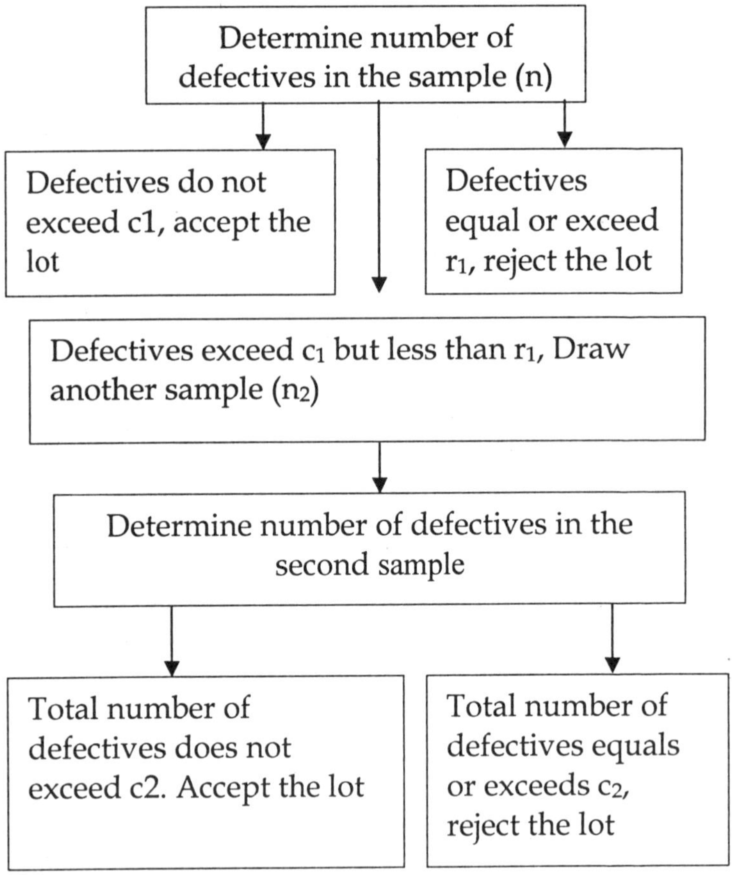

4.6.5 Multiple Sampling Plan: A multiple sampling procedure is based on the pre determined number of samples to be drawn for deciding acceptance of the lot. These plans give a psychological advantage to the supplier a second chance (as in case of double sampling) or more number of chances in multiple sampling. It however involves higher cost of inspection and more administrative requirement.

4.6.6 Switching Procedure: The system also provides for a switching procedure which depends entirely on the performance of the vendor—the quality of the supplies received over a period of time. The result of the normal inspection procedure dictates either to tighten the procedure or to relax further.

4.6.7 Normal to Reduce: When normal inspection is in effect and the performance is consistently good reduced inspection shall follow subject to satisfying the following:

1. Preceding 10 lots have been accepted on normal inspection.
2. Number of defects in the preceding 10 samples is less than equal to the number indicated in the table.

4.6.8 Normal to Tightened: Tightened inspection shall be instituted when 2 out of 5 consecutive lot/batches are rejected (resubmitted supply to be ignored) and when 5 consecutive batches are considered acceptable, the normal procedure is restored.

In such a case, the production is at steady state and the reduced inspection procedure shall be reverted to normal in case a lot is rejected or the vendor's supply/production becomes irregular or there are other compelling conditions that warrant normal inspection.

The inspection plan also should also include the following:

A. Process Inspection: The objective of process inspection is to prevent manufacture of parts/components of unacceptable quality (defects) being produced and delivered to customers—external and internal. The process inspection is three types, namely first-piece inspection, patrol inspection and assembly line inspection.

The first-piece inspection is conducted for the detection of any systemic defect that may arise due to faulty machine setting, wrong tools/jigs by inadvertence or otherwise. The defects in the first-piece inspection signals to stop the manufacturing process and look for causes systematically—from raw material specification, manufacturing instruction, performance of the operator to problems with the machine or the tools used.

During patrol inspection, the quality inspectors randomly check important parameters for conformance and in the event of defects in a sample, the process is stopped for identification of causes and their rectification so that defective parts are not produced any more.

B. Final Inspection: The final inspection is carried out on completion of the manufacture of an item—component, sub-assembly, assembly or a finished product and prior to dispatching the product to the customers. The objective is to prevent defective product leaving the plant. Usually, the product is subject to test for conformance of performance, safety requirement and aesthetic appearance.

The performance testing involves subjecting the item to normal use including type testing that the product operates satisfactorily. While the appearance is a visual check, the safety requirement calls for strict compliance as per standards, for example current leakage test is critical for electrically operated equipment.

C. Inspection Instruction: The inspection instruction also need to be prepared precisely with clear quality characteristics, type of measuring instrument to be used, sample size and periodicity (as per readily available sample plan, accepted by the industry) including AQL.

4.7 Reporting

A company should have detailed information on the defects, their causes and remedies. The technical nature of data helps managers to look up in future as a guideline. The senior management however is more concerned with report on costs relating to waste/scrap, rework etc. and the cost trend over a period of time. A system of collecting data for each product unit on its journey through initial to final stage, along with defects noted and repair done are essential. A system of reporting meant for different usage also need to be introduced, for example, periodic report for the top management reflecting failure costs and comparing with the previous period; technical report for managers for dissemination to operators and vendors by way of feedback.

4.7.1 Principles: The principles of executive reporting broadly include the following:

1. The report should be based on facts.
2. Data need to be summarized category-wise (output during the period, defect type, failure cost, appraisal cost).
3. Comparison with relevant previous period (week, month) for analysing trend.
4. Report needs to be prepared immediately, as delay renders the report irrelevant.
5. It should be precise, to the point and include suggestion for action with rationale.

4.7.2 Cost Analysis: Periodic analysis of quality cost and savings accrued from the quality efforts over a period of time is necessary. It evidences the efficiency of the improvement process and the management including the workers are satisfied that the company gains: top management takes interest and workers are motivated.

4.7.3 Computer Aided System: The recent trend is towards computer based system for inspection instruction, data record and reporting. The offers a paperless inspection plan that can be used to create inspection routines without need for a traditional blueprint. As part of the process of improving inspection planning and increasing efficiency in part programming, some developers have improved measurement and inspection software.

4.8 The Kaizen Approach

Post war, Japan undertook the daunting task of rebuilding its economy and the Economic and Scientific Section (ESS) developed a training film, titled 'Improvement in Four Steps' (*Kaizen eno YonDankai)* to introduce the Three TWI 'J' programme—job instruction, job methods, job relations—that paved the way for formal introduction of K*aizen* in Japan. Kaizen has its roots to the Japanese words *Kai*-change and *Zen*-good. It refers to the philosophy or practices that focus upon continuous incremental improvement of processes in manufacturing, engineering, supporting business processes including people. [11] The concept focuses heavily on continuous improvement of a business organization that includes both people and process. For the pioneering effort of introducing and implementing Kaizen in Japan, the Emperor of Japan awarded the Second Order Medal of the Sacred Treasure to Dr. Deming in 1960. Consequently, the Union of Japanese Scientist and Engineering (JUSE) instituted the annual Deming Prizes for achievements in quality and dependability of products in Japan.

To begin with, the application of *Kaizen* concept was limited to manufacturing industry and with its success, the concept is now applied to healthcare, government, banking, and many other sectors. [12] When used in the business sense and applied to the workplace, kaizen refers to activities that continually improve all functions, and involves all employees from the CEO to the assembly line workers. It also applies to processes, such as purchasing and logistics that cross organizational boundaries into the supply chain.

The format for Kaizen can be individual, small group or large group. At Toyota Plant, the practice was to gain improvement at work stations or local area involving small group for improving their work environment and productivity. The supervisor generally guides the group on Kaizen process. In a total quality setting, all operators and processor supervisors are expected to stop their moving production line in case of any abnormality for identifying the problem and suggesting an improvement to resolve the abnormality. The practice initiates a kaizen and the organization accrues long-term gain. [13]

In modern usage, a focused kaizen that is designed to address a particular issue over the course of a week is referred to as a "kaizen blitz" or "kaizen event".

The development inspired all and the Toyota culture became the quality culture in a business organization. It has proved to be very powerful approach for attaining quality, reducing waste and meeting customer expectations.

The key elements of kaizen are quality, effort, involvement of all employees, willingness to change, and communication. And for achieving these goals, the practice lays priority on the following:

1. Customer focus.
2. Management commitment.
3. Management-employee co-operation.
4. Employee involvement.
5. Team work.
6. Implementing total quality for improvement of productivity.

4.8.1 Implementation of the Concept: The starting point for implementing the concept is to recognize the need. Kaizen emphasizes problem awareness and provides clues for identifying them. Imai suggests five-step plan for successfully implementing this concept for systemic and continuous improvement. These are *seiri, seiton, seiso, seiketsu, and shitsuke* which mean straighten-up, put things in order, cleanup, personal cleanliness and discipline.

The widely used management tools are 'five Ws and the H' and their use encourages employees to look at the existing process and ask for improvement:

1. Who—who is doing it? Who should be doing it?
2. What—what is being done? What should be done?
3. Where—where is it being done? Where should it be done?
4. When—when is it being done? When should it be done?
5. Why—why is it being done? Why do it that way?
6. How—how is it being done? How should it be done?

It also focuses on the key factors contributing to the process (five Ms): man, machine, material, method and measurement.

4.8.2 The Concept in Practice: The underlying system of Kaizen can be summarised as continuous improvement of all aspects in an organization with the involvement of employees at all levels, at all time and forever. Kaizen is a daily activity, the purpose of which goes beyond simple productivity improvement. And when done correctly, the process humanizes the workplace, eliminates overly hard work 'muri', and teaches people how to perform experiments on their work using the scientific method and learn how to spot and eliminate waste in business processes. In all, the process suggests a humanized approach to workers and to increasing productivity: "The idea is to nurture the company's human resources as much as it is to praise and encourage participation in kaizen activities". Successful implementation requires "the participation of employees at all levels in the process of improvement".

4.8.3 Benefits of Kaizen Approach: It yields excellent results in the form of compound productivity improvement by improving standardized activities and processes. Kaizen aims at eliminating waste and there by cost reduction and increase in profit. It also provides an enabling work environment with willing participation of all.

4.9 Benchmarking

Benchmarking is the process of identifying 'best practice' in relation to both products and the processes by which those products are created and delivered. The search for 'best practice' can takes place both within a particular industry and also in other industries (for example—are there lessons to be learned from other industries?) where some of the processes are similar. The objective of benchmarking is to understand and evaluate the firm's current position of a business in relation to better performing ones and to identify areas and means of performance improvement.

4.9.1 Definition: Benchmarking is defined as the process of measuring for the comparison of an organization's operations or its internal process against those of the best-in-class performer from inside or outside of the industry. Dimensions typically measured are quality, time and cost. Improvements from learning mean doing things better, faster, and cheaper.

It is finding the secret of the success of any business from the existing process in the manufacture and learn from the information to improve upon the existing process performance. It is not to be misunderstood with competitive analysis, which involves comparing against competitor's product or service-its features, quality and price.

The term benchmarking was first used by cobblers to measure people's feet for shoes. They would place someone's foot on a "bench" and mark it out to make the pattern for the shoes. Benchmarking is most used to measure performance using a specific indicator (cost per unit of measure, productivity per unit of measure, cycle time of production per unit of measure or defects per unit of measure) resulting in a matrix of performance which is subsequently compared with industry average and that of the better performing units. The important aspects are as follows:

1. Benchmarking is a respected means of identifying the weaker process that require improvement.
2. It involves comparing with the best-in-class and getting required information from them with their consent.
3. The objective is to improve in complete awareness that a specific process has been proved mere efficient in another plant.
4. It concerns processes and practices.

4.9.2 Benchmarking Process: Benchmarking involves looking outward (outside a particular business organisation, industry, region or country) to examine how others achieve their performance levels and to emulate the processes they use. In this way benchmarking helps explain the processes behind excellent performance. When the lessons learnt from a benchmarking exercise are applied appropriately, they facilitate improved performance in critical functions within an organisation or in key areas of the business environment.

The technique which has been initially used to compare existing corporate strategies with those in practice else where for achieving the best possible performance has recently been extended to the compare process performance in respect of a technical product. This process is usually referred to as "Technical Benchmarking" or "Product Benchmarking". Its use is particularly well developed within the automotive industry ("Automotive Benchmarking"), where it is vital to design products that match precise user expectations, at minimum possible cost, by applying the best technologies available worldwide. Many data are obtained by fully disassembling existing cars and their systems. Such analyses were initially carried out in-house by car makers and their suppliers. However, as they are expensive, they are increasingly outsourced to companies specialized in this area. Indeed, outsourcing has enabled a drastic decrease in costs for each company (by cost sharing) and the development of very efficient tools. The various types of benchmarking presently in vogue include the following:

1. **Process Benchmarking:** The initiating firm focuses its observation and investigation of business processes with a clear objective of identifying and observing the best practices from one or more benchmark firms. Activity analysis will be required where the focus is to benchmark cost and efficiency; increasingly applied to back-office processes where outsourcing may be a consideration.
2. **Financial Benchmarking:** Performing a financial analysis and comparing the results in an effort to assess a company's overall competitiveness and productivity.
3. **Benchmarking from an Investor Perspective:** Extending the benchmarking universe to compare to peer companies that can be considered alternative investment opportunities from the perspective of an investor.
4. **Performance Benchmarking:** Allows the initiator firm

to assess their competitive position by comparing products and services with those of target firms.

5. **Product Benchmarking:** The process of designing new products or upgrades to current ones. This process can sometimes involve reverse engineering which is examining competitors' products to find strengths and weaknesses.
6. **Strategic Benchmarking:** Involves observing how others compete. This type is usually not industry specific, meaning it is best to look at other industries.
7. **Functional Benchmarking:** A company will focus its benchmarking on a single function to improve the operation of that particular function. Complex functions such as human resources, finance and accounting and information and communication technology are unlikely to be directly comparable in cost and efficiency terms and may need to be disaggregated into processes to make valid comparison.
8. **Best-in-class Benchmarking:** Involves studying the leading competitor or the company that best carries out a specific function.
9. **Operational Benchmarking:** Embraces everything from staffing and productivity to office flow and analysis of procedures performed.
10. **Energy Benchmarking:** Developing an accurate model of a building's energy consumption with the purpose of measuring reductions in usage.

4.9.3 Implementation: The key feature for the implementation and adoption of best-in-class practice would include the following:

1. Benchmarking requires top management commitment.
2. The organization must understand its process properly and identify strong as well as weak processes.
3. Select the process which is to be benchmarked (that requires improvement).
4. Form benchmarking team.

5. Research best-in-class from within or outside the industry.
6. Compare the results and processes of those studied (the "targets") to learn how well the targets perform and, more importantly, how they do it.
7. Select benchmarking partner, enter into agreement.
8. Collect required data, including training for process improvement.
9. Analyze the information.
10. Plan for implementation.
11. Implement the required change.
12. Monitor performance.
13. Update the process—continue the cycle.

4.9.4 Prerequisite for Successful Implementation: The benefits from the introduction of any new system in an organization could be derived when the there is conducive environment, proper attitude, required skill and more importantly the will and commitment of the management—an essential qualifying attribute. The management should be open to new ideas. Psychological and attitudinal mind-set sometime pose problem for change and requires skilful handling by leadership.

It is mandatory that the company understands fully its product, service, processes and practice; analyzes them to identify the weak areas, internally or with the help of quality consultants; selects a suitable partner and sincerely implements following expert advice. It is to be kept in mind that best-in-class is a dynamic and ever changing concept. With sweeping development of technology and innovation, processes are being improved over a short span and to take advantage of the experience, efforts-allocation of resource, innovation through research and development— are required to stay up to date. It is a continuous improvement process. [14]

4.9.5 Costs: The costs involved in benchmarking could be grouped in the following three main categories:

1. **Visit Costs:** It includes travel costs, hotel rooms, meals, a token gift and lost working time.

2. **Time Costs:** Members of the benchmarking team will be investing time in researching problems, finding exceptional companies to study, visiting units of interest and implementing the project. This takes them away from their regular job for part of each day so additional staff might be required.
3. **Benchmarking Database Costs:** Organizations that institutionalize benchmarking into their normal practice find it is useful to create and maintain a database of best practices based on their experience.

The cost of benchmarking can substantially be reduced through utilizing the vast internet resources that have sprung up over the last few years. The aim to capture benchmarks and best practices from manufacturing plants, industry sectors and countries to make the benchmarking process much quicker and cheaper.

Benchmarking should not be considered a one-off exercise. To be effective, it must become an ongoing, integral part of an improvement process with the goal of keeping abreast of ever-improving best practice. Benchmarking is a technique applied to the total quality process. It is becoming increasingly popular with companies marketing or intending to market their product and services in international market. The organization, especially the managers interested in quality improvement need to know about the system, practice, its benefits and how to go about it.

4.10 Just-in-Time Manufacturing

'Just-in-Time' (JIT) suggests 'getting materials delivered when needed', there by implicitly conveying that the producers/suppliers to keep the materials inventory for supply on demand. This is a common perception, but the statement demonstrates only a limited understanding of the JIT concept.

4.10.1 What is JIT? Just-in-time is producing only what is needed, when it is needed and in the quantity that is needed. A manufacturing unit following JIT procedure does not overproduce at any step, neither finished product nor intermediate component or subassembly. Thus, there is no storage of materials, no spoilage, waste, no money locked in. The elimination of these wastes alone makes JIT the most powerful manufacturing concept to come along since Henry Ford's assembly line of 1913 (Goetsch and Davis, 1994:514). JIT is considered an important technique for continuous improvement as the practice eliminates wastes, improves competitiveness of product and service and as a result accomplishes better customer satisfaction.

Kiichiro Toyoda, the founder chairman of Toyota, Japan, greatly influenced by Ford's automation initiated planning for assembly line at his plant intending that things be done exactly on schedule. It increased production, but generated huge inventory. After the World War, Taiichi Ohno with the support of Eiji Toyoda developed the JIT philosophy and applied it at Toyota plant. Ohno notes that 'in broad industries, such as automobile manufacturing, it is best to have various parts arrive alongside the assembly line just-in-time'. To Ohno, the mass production system inherently overproduces at every stage which costs to the company and need to be eliminated for achieving cost control. [15]

Mass production is a push system. Production as per the forecast based on historical data which often goes wrong in the dynamic market scenario. JIT, on the other hand is a pull system. The production schedule is not based on forecast but with demands from the customer. The demand is placed on the final assembly which pulls the demand on the preceding process and the cycle is complete with finished product delivered. The problems of the machine are reduced with efficient preventive maintenance and problems including redundancy of the processes are eliminated by thoroughly understanding the process and applying SPC to keep the process in control and continuous improvement for total quality.

He identified seven wastes that should be eliminated to

gain cost advantage and these are:

1. Overproduction.
2. Waiting (time) for man and material.
3. Moving work in progress back and forth in the plant (unnecessary transportation).
4. Inefficient or redundant process.
5. Excessive inventory.
6. Non-value added movement.
7. Producing defective goods.

4.10.2 Benefits of JIT: Mass production system emphasizes the need to keep the assembly line moving or the process flows to achieve production target, even at the cost of high inventory cost for any contingency that may arise. JIT procedure however does not allow any buffer stock of parts with full awareness that one missing part or a single fault in any machine may result the production line to stop. The JIT approach adequately takes care of this and it is its strength. In practice, the people involved rely on anticipating, developing and immediately solving the problems and the operators are always in focus.

A comparative distinction of the traditional factory engaged in mass production and a total quality factory is:

Traditional factory: line stops because of machine breakdown, part or operator not available:

1. Attitude: disturbance in production line to be avoided at any cost.
2. Reaction: get the line moving and try to correct later.
3. Result: production quantity achieved, quality spared.

Total quality factory: line may stop because of process problem found by operator.

1. Attitude: It presents an opportunity for improvement.
2. Reaction: To determine cause and eliminate defect
3. Result: Immediate production loss but long-term gain, i.e. quality output from improved process.

David Lu in '*Kanban: Just-in-Time at Toyota*' presents a true story from Toyota how the unit trying to follow JIT system attains overall gain where as another of old school shows only immediate production in quantity (1990:73).

4.11 Kanban

Kanban is the Japanese word for card. Ohno developed it for maintaining the flow of part and component through out the process as required. It is to signal pull through the system. Simply put, when a process uses parts/material, it issues a *kanban* to the preceding process for production and the flow of material is ensured. The system may evolve a number of forms as per the process requirement; for example a process produces a part/subassembly and places it on the marked area for the succeeding workstation and when it is utilized, the *kanban* square becomes empty and signals production to fill the space. Thus the system pulls. As a result, the inventory of finished goods, work-in-process and inputs are minimized.

4.11.1 Successful Implementation: The important aspects that need serious consideration for the system to be effective are:

1. Factory organization: the lay out of shops and machines are designed in keeping with the natural flow of the manufacturing process, so that there is no unnecessary movement of man or material. The flow is smooth, unobstructed.
2. Education and Training: it is essential that the workers and supervisors involved develop skill, understand and appreciate the system and apply objectively.
3. Developing team spirit: though individual efficiency is important, the coordinated effort is essential for success because all employees in an organization are links in the same chain and are interdependent.
4. Kanban: it is key to success of the system, which *inter-alia* necessitates the following:

- Stabilize and rationalize process flow.
- Adhere to kanban instructions.
- Smooth the production load.

- Produce only the exact quantity and of required quality (defective parts should not be put to the system).
- Subsequent process to draw what is needed, when needed.

JIT is the most powerful technique available for reducing cycle time. In fact, shorter the production cycle time, lower the production cost. Short cycle time improves a factory's ability to respond quickly the changing needs of customers. [16]

End Notes

1. A typical check sheet is divided into regions, and marks made in different regions have different significance.
2. The operator feels that he or his action is not being policed. It also saves inspection time.
3. Ishikawa too points out that 'while there are many cause factors, the truly important ones, the cause factors which will sharply influence effects are not many'.
4. Statistics is considered to be a mathematical science pertaining to the collection, organization, analysis, interpretation or explanation, and presentation of data.
5. Readers may refer to *'Quality Control Handbook'* or *'Statistics'* for further information on the subject.
6. Shewhart's book *'The Economic Control of Quality of Manufactured Product'* of 1931 is a pioneering work.
7. Normally a fishbone diagram is used to examine special causes and how they impact the process.
8. Mean (x) standard deviation (□) are measures of central tendency in statistics.
9. ISO 2859-4:2002 establishes the sampling plans and the procedures that can be used to assess whether the quality level of an entity (lot, process) conforms to a declared standard specification. The sampling plans have been devised so as to obtain a risk of less than 5 percent of a correct declared quality level.
10. The lot size determines the sample size (n), the accepted number of defects (r) in the sample. Standard charts with lot size, 'n' and 'r' are available in *'Quality Control Handbook'*.
11. Imai in *'kaizen: The Key to Japan's Competitive Success'* states, 'The strategy is the single most important concept in Japanese management-the key to Japanese competitive success.'

12. Anthony Robbins and Robert Maurer have popularized application of the kaizen principles into personnel development.
13. Liker and Meier in '*The Toyota Way Fieldbook*' Meier discuss the kaizen blitz and kaizen burst (or kaizen event) approaches to continuous improvement. A kaizen blitz, or rapid improvement, is a focused activity on a particular process or activity. The basic concept is to identify and quickly remove waste. Another approach is that of the kaizen burst, a specific kaizen activity on a particular process in the value stream.
14. Motorola, one of the Malcolm Baldrige award winner company has found that even after achieving best-in-class, there is much to gain through continued Benchmarking (Goetsch and Davis, 1994:417).
15. In this context, readers may like to refer to the concept of 'lean manufacturing'.
16. Goetsch and Davis in '*Introduction to Total quality*' note that 'the less time the product spends in the production cycle, the less chance there is for damage.

5

Evolution of Quality Systems

Chapter 2 provided an overview of the development of quality concepts by the pioneering efforts of many thinkers, quality experts in keeping with the changing needs of the industry for attaining product quality. The defining characteristics of quality seem to be more and more oriented towards customer satisfaction. And in order to achieve this, the business and industry strive to fine-tune operating processes and associated systems with deployment of appropriate tools and techniques (refer Chapter 4). In this chapter, it is attempted to chronicle the development of quality systems, and practices for managing quality, most of which are universally applied in industry. Since developments of various related aspects have been on a parallel way in different locations, a systemic presentation is preferred to time-scheduling.

5.1 Quality Control

An approach to controlling quality of a product can be traced to the development of human civilization, when man learnt to make a product and use it for specific purpose. Around one million BCE, give or take a few centuries, man first began to fashion and use stone tools for hunting and survival. [1] The individual skill in making products dominated until 8000 BCE, when assembling began that required fitting a hole-the first use of interchangeable parts on a limited basis.

Early efforts to control the quality of production has been documented in case of a civil engineering project for building the Great Pyramid of Giza from specifications that required the four sides of the base to be perpendicular to within 3.5 arc seconds. The Royal government seems to have taken interest in quality in purchasing material. For this reason, King John of England appointed William Wrotham to report about the construction and repair of ships. Centuries later, Samuel Pepys, Secretary to the British Admiralty, appointed multiple such overseers to check on quality during procurement.

Prior to the Industrial Revolution, the skilled craftsman used to control the quality of their own creation. Working conditions then were arguably more conducive to professional pride and quality was more subjective based on aesthetic appeal. The craft era that extended from the Stone Age up to and overlapping Industrial Revolution gradually ceased with the development of batch or mass production with assembly line. The extensive division of labour and mechanization that resulted from the development of technology led to a system in which large number of people performed various functions simultaneously for the manufacture of parts/components for the assembly of a complex item. It necessitated defining specification for production and measurement for controlling the quality of a product in order that it is as per specification for meeting customer's requirement: external (final product) and internal (for subsequent operation). The conformance to specification was ensured by inspection under the supervision of the quality control department of the company.

5.1.1 Testing for Conformance: Quality control is a formal and a structured method of testing. In principle, quality control describes the directed use of testing to measure the output of a production process as against a specified standard. Testing involves a complete range of measurement, from simple visual test for evaluating breakages to test of critical parameters by sophisticated equipment, as the product specification demands. Measurement is essential for ascertaining whether the output is within the allowable tolerance limits and if not, rectification required for stabilizing the process. The system comprises three components:

1. The standard or objective specification.
2. Means for measuring to compare actual result with the

specified limits.

3. Using the test results from the measurement for improvement.

It is, thus, a superset of testing, although it often used synonymously with testing.

5.1.2 Limitations: The procedure for quality control by inspection at times imposes certain psychological barriers: the operators perceive the quality inspectors assigned to take samples, measure and record results of measurement as policing. The total quality approach overcomes such a situation by promoting self-measurement, self-correction for improvement by a system that assigns the operators to take sample, measure the output, record the data in the control chart and initiate action as required. It is motivating for the operators and easy in implementation.

Yet another way of looking at the difference between testing and quality control is to consider the difference between a test as an event and a test as a part of a system. The initial years of quality initiative was based mainly on inspection on the factory floor. To begin with, quality control involved testing of products to uncover defects and separating defective part, component or a complete item from the lot in order that the customers receive the good product that meets specification. It subsequently changed to reporting to management for taking decision, either to allow or deny the release, in addition to taking necessary steps to improve and the stabilize production process and associated processes, to avoid, or at least minimize, the problems that led to the defects in the first place.

The process ensured improvement in 'fitness for use' for the internal as well as external customers. The procedure however remained limited to post production stage. It was found to be inadequate because reduction of defects during the manufacturing stage by corrective action was beyond the scope of the system. It is also noted that in certain occasions, despite pursuing quality control approach in all its sincerity, sales decrease. This is due to the fact that, either the original specification does not reflect the correct quality requirements (improper design) for instance, the parameters of a pressure vessel should include not only the material and dimensions, but also operating process, environmental, requirements for safety, reliability and maintainability which are to be incorporated by design. And even in the event of defects in output despite correct operation, it is to be confirmed whether the process is capable of meeting specification.

In order to take care of this requirement, a noteworthy development for the improvement of the quality control system was introduction of statistical quality control (SQC) using sample inspection and control charts.

5.2 Statistical Quality Control (SQC)

Traditional SQC in manufacturing operations usually proceed by randomly sampling and testing a fraction of the output. Variances in critical tolerances are continuously tracked by planned inspection and assignable causes are remedied immediately. [2] It eliminates occurrence of further defective output. Many organizations use statistical process control to bring the organization to Six Sigma levels of quality; in other words, the likelihood of an unexpected failure is confined to six standard deviations on the normal distribution. The probability becomes less than four one-millionth. The sampling technique also helps to overcome the situation that in cases, 100 percent inspection is not practically feasible in addition to reducing the cost of quality control. A detailed discussion on control chart, its application and usefulness as an effective quality tool is available in chapter 4.

To sum up, statistical quality control is a method by which manufacturing companies are in a position to continuously review the quality of the output. It offers an insight to the problems, the related cause of variation and the parameters to be controlled to get the production process stable. This approach places high emphasis on the following three aspects:

1. Elements such as process management, measurement for actual performance and integrity criteria including evaluation of process capability.
2. Competence of workers, such as knowledge, skills, experience and training.
3. Soft elements, such as personnel integrity, confidence, organizational culture, motivation, team spirit and quality relationships.

The quality of the outputs is at risk if any of these three aspects is deficient in any way. And in order to accomplish the goal, total quality is considered most appropriate.

5.3 Total Quality

The origin of company wide quality control or total quality is usually ascribed to Japan's search for improvement during the post-War period when Japanese goods were regarded synonymous with cheap and poor quality product. Japanese industry was particularly receptive to ideas that would help attaining superior quality of product for a number of reasons and significantly to achieve:

5.3.1 Market Expansion: The single most important factor was the need for promoting exports. Beside price which could be achieved through relative labour cost advantage, quality improvement was considered crucial. The gains accrued are elimination of defects, production to specification, and eventual reduction in cost.

5.3.2 Achieving Excellence: The quality concepts developed by the western quality experts like Deming and Juran were readily accepted by Japanese industry rather than the American. They received a willing audience for experimenting new ideas such as statistical quality control and other problem-solving techniques. This could be due to the long established Japanese tradition of fine craftsmanship [3] or their eagerness to improve for achieving excellence in production.

Quality development education progressed fast in Japan

with the support of the senior management of industry in addition to the Union of Japanese Scientists and Engineers (JUSE) and Japanese Management Association (JMA) at national level. The industries, in their quest for excellence in quality standards achieved phenomenal success leaving behind American and other western industries in important sectors like automobiles, consumer electronics and the like. Amazed at the development trend and realizing that the market share was on the decline, Ford Motor Company took the help of Deming to start a quality initiative afresh. The programme was for application of the quality tools and techniques developed in the West as well as in Japan in industry for improving quality of output.

The concept of 'company wide quality control' or 'total quality' (TQ) with the focus on management and people came to the fore during 1980s. The practice of quality management aimed at enlisting the cooperation of the entire organization, i.e. all departments: market study, product development, procurement, manufacturing, quality, marketing and service including administration, finance and employees at all levels.

The definition of TQ endorsed by the Total Quality Forum aptly states that it is 'a people focused management system that aims at continual increase in customer satisfaction at continually lower cost. TQ is a total system approach and an integral part of high level strategy. It works horizontally across functions and departments, involving all employees, top to bottom and extends backwards to include the supply chain and the customer chain'. [4]

The concept encompasses a set of philosophies by which management system can be directed to realization of organizational objectives ensuring comprehensive action for customer satisfaction including maximizing gains for all stakeholders-shareholders, employees, customers and suppliers. It is an attempt not only to make better products but also searching better ways of making.

Total quality is an approach to doing business that

attempts to maximize the competitiveness of an organization through continuous improvement of quality of product/service, people, process and environment. Concentrating on quality would ultimately improve both productivity and profitability. In essence, it is total because it covers every process, every job and every person involved in the organization. The process covers collection of information by marketing department regarding consumer needs and preferences, research and design to incorporate collected data in product features, manufacturing as per specification, quality control, after sales service, accounting, human resource development, vendor selection and procurement.

It is essential to have quality in design rather than quality in production alone. [5] The priority of each job in quality is related to all functions—buying, producing, measuring, repairing and maintenance in right manner. And it aims at creating an environment where each person from top to bottom, irrespective of the department strives for excellence. The management is in a position to integrate the whole organization, especially the departments directly or indirectly contributing to product quality and alter the basic philosophy including operating strategy in order that quality becomes an important component in the common language of communication for all.

Six organizational issues point to the need to focus while managing organizational structure and change processes for total quality: international competition, external as well as internal customer needs, workforce diversity and expectations, information technology and knowledge requirement and the need for development of world-class organizational culture (Lindsay and Petrick, 1997:5). Ackoff (1993) however, points out that, 'managing total quality requires a revision of management and restructuring of the organization involved. TQ requires a revolution, not reform. The challenge is to make it and make it bloodless.'

In this context, Lindsay and Petrick (1997) present a

'House of Total Quality' model [6] as a comprehensive frame of reference for integrating key aspects of organization design and operation. It consists of six components:

1. The roof or superstructure represents four organizational subsystems—management, technical, social and educational systems.
2. The four pillars of quality—customer satisfaction, continuous improvement, speaking with facts and respects for people.
3. The four foundations—strategy management, process management, project management and individual task management.
4. The four corner stones—strategic planning, process planning, project planning and task planning.
5. The mortar of deployment for holding the structure in shape and providing strength.
6. The ethical work culture.

Total quality has been widely accepted and 'regarded as a major innovation in management practice of the 1980s and has been hailed as a thought revolution in quality management. (Ishikawa, 1985:1) By mid-1980s, quality management appeared to be more well developed in manufacturing industries than in service sector and has primary association with quality tools and techniques that led to newer development. The introduction of 'market' in the organization, that is the concept of internal customer, led to breakdown the difference and latent conflict within that sometimes arise due to occupational and functional segmentation. It integrates the whole organization, from the market research, design and development, production to after sales department for pursuing a focused objective.

For establishing a total quality organization and improving the manufacturing systems, integration of men, machine and materials were considered a prerequisite. While machine and material were taken care of by technical and management techniques, Japan developed novel approach for empowerment of people in order to ensure their involvement and commitment. It involves:

1. Management and motivation of employees for their sincere involvement in continuous improvement.
2. Improvement of the process by creative application of knowledge, tools and techniques.
3. Control of the process by operating personnel to remain productive.

Japanese industry achieved the objective by the introduction of quality circle in industry and it helped, to a large extent, to enhance the scope for establishing a total quality organization.

5.4 Quality Circle

Post-War, General Douglas Mac Arthur was the commander of the occupational forces in Japan. He took up initiative for imparting quality awareness among Japanese industry to help them improve their product quality for increasing trade essential for economic progress. He invited eminent quality experts like Deming and Juran, who found Japan welcoming to implement their new approach in industry for achieving its objective: improvement of quality of product as soon as possible. Japan was in a hurry. The industry imported required technology to have access to the technical details of production and blended with employees' involvement in the process by proper education, training including rewards that induce competition. The environment was for change towards better. An innovative approach 'Quality Circle' was developed to supplement the efforts in realizing objective.

Quality circle was first introduced as a system for improving product quality at the Nippon Wireless and Telegraph Company in Japan in 1962 and Kaoru Ishikawa has been credited as its creator. Some believe that the term, quality circle owes its origin to the concept of 'Plan-Do-Check-Act' (PDCA) circle developed by W. Edwards Deming. Within a year, it spread to more than 35 other companies and by 1978, it is claimed, more than one million quality circles involving some 10 million Japanese workers were functional. It benefited Japanese industry in many meaningful ways: improved human relations, better understanding of the job requirement, product and process improvement with direct contribution of employees. It also acts as a great motivator.

The precept of quality circle is concern for people. It is based on the broad premise that:

1. People are basically intelligent, capable and want to do a good job.
2. They need education, training, encouragement and good environment.
3. They want to participate in the decision making that affects their job.
4. Employees in the organization expect full information regarding the goal, management action, the problems, if any to participate for accomplishment, and also to be recognized for their contribution as a part of the system.

5.4.1 Structure and Functioning: Quality circle is formed by a small group of 6 to 12 employees engaged in similar activity. It is composed of workers and supervisors involved in day to day functioning and fully aware of the production process. The group chooses its leader, but it is generally the team leader.

The system begins with a system of training of the members by experts from within the company or with the help of outside consultant (usually designated as facilitators) who are qualified on the application of quality tools, techniques required to analyze and solve work-related problems or industrial relations specialists trained in human relations or specialists on the basic skills of information gathering, statistics and analysis, identification of causes by the application of relevant tools and solution generation.

Quality circles function as formal groups. The members meet at least once a week on company time. The group is free to select any topic they believe is of importance to the organization, for example, tackling problems faced during production, reducing time for a job, operator's convenience and safety to wastage reduction. The issues relating to salary and terms and conditions of work are beyond its scope as there are other channels for redressal.

The group voluntarily meets together on a regular basis. Every member is actively engaged in the innovative application of proven techniques in their respective work areas for analyzing and solving work related problems that come in the way of achieving and sustaining excellence. The members being the part of the system, they are naturally aware of the problem in greater details. The group presents its suggestions to the management for consideration and implementation which ultimately results in the improvement of performance of the company. The workers take pride for their creative suggestion being implemented and a competitive spirit ensues.

5.4.2 Benefits: Business organization usually accrues many benefits from the implementation of quality circle and the important among these include the following:

1. Quality circle has been proved to be an effective 'way of capturing the creative and innovative power that lies within the work force' for improvement in product design, manufacturing process including improvement in working environment, safety and health.
2. It has the advantage of continuity: the circle remains intact from project to project.
3. The concept has been accepted all over the world as a very effective system to improve the quality of work life. With introduction of assembly line for mass production, individual workers have been treated like robots-to work in a specific manner for a specific duration, and the monotony of work has been a deterrent in the motivational propensity. The development and practice of this approach—working in small groups with opportunity for all to contribute and get recognition has resulted in an

alternative to the dehumanizing concept of the division of labour bringing back the concept of craftsmanship, which when used in group form (as is the case with quality circles) proved to be overwhelmingly powerful.

4. It enriches the lives of the workers, creating harmony and high performance in the workplace.
5. Though the share of the cost benefit of any improvements resulting from quality circle is not usually distributed to the members directly, a proportion of the savings made is spent on improvements to the work environment.

Quality circle has proved to be an effective group technique and is certainly a finite part of a much broader total quality effort. Its astonishing and unique achievement in industry became an eye-opener to the world. Industries from all over the world started visiting Japan to know how they have achieved such magical results in such a short span. Most of the Japanese products are topping the world in quality and productivity ranking. [7]

When the technique was implemented in the United States in early 1970s, it was not proved successful. Sandholm (1983) considers such outcome has been due mainly to the fact that, 'the West is essentially copying the Japanese idea of quality circle and overlooking firm's vital quality infrastructure'. In Japan quality circles have always been an integral part of a companywide approach to quality where as in the US, it was more directed to be a fault-finding, rather than an exercise for improvement. The concept perhaps was not properly understood.

The quality circle in industry did spread world over. It gained popularity in most East Asian countries, China and Japan. According to some estimates, there were more than 20 million quality circles in China a few years back. In India, the concept was introduced by companies with Japanese collaboration and spread to others by 1990s. The Quality Circle Forum of India (QCFI) promotes such activities.

Though quality circle served its purpose to get employees'

involvement for better performance, it was found inadequate as its scope was limited to workplace within a department. And in search for a management system that takes care of the organization as a whole, companywide quality approach emerged. A comparison of total quality *vis-à-vis* quality circle would reveal the limitations of quality circle:

1. The scope-companywide as against department.
2. The objective-product quality improvement in place of employee understanding.
3. The working-it was compulsory, as against voluntary.
4. The approach-top-down instead of bottom-up for quality circle.

5.5 Quality Assurance

The approach to achieve product quality with application of quality tools and techniques remain confined to the shop floor practice. The operator could identify the assignable causes of variation of the production process, but could not reveal certain quality problems associated with other departments contributing to quality. This led to subsequent development of different approaches and the most important one is 'quality assurance that includes the concept of cost of quality, total quality control (TQC), reliability engineering and zero defects (Garvin, 1988:12-14).

And in the context of Juran's affirmation that, 'quality improvement encompasses both improving fitness for use and reducing the level of defects and errors' a structured programme for managing quality became inevitable and quality assurance (QA) came into practice. It assumed relevance as the companies expanded their activity and the stakes rose.

The objective was to improve and stabilize production bringing all the associated processes under control to avoid, or at least minimize the problems that led to the defects in the first place. Quality control however continues to be an essential component of the quality system, for it ensures planned measurement and test for conformance. In addition, it also provides data on real-time basis for analysis using appropriate quality tools and techniques. QC activities thus are integral to the overall methodologies developed and used to prevent errors and defects from arising.

Quality assurance was initially introduced during World War II when munitions were inspected and tested for defects after they were made. Today's quality assurance systems emphasize catching defects before they get into the final product. In manufacturing and construction activities, these business practices should be as per the models for quality assurance defined by the International Standards contained in the ISO 9000 series specifications for quality systems. Two key principles characterize QA:

1. **Fit for use:** The product should be suitable for the intended purpose.
2. **Right first time:** Mistakes should be eliminated from the design stage along with quality planning and stabilizing production process.

It entails introducing proper system for ensuring quality of inputs: raw materials, components, sub-assemblies including associated systems and processes.

Quality assurance refers to a program for the systematic monitoring and evaluation of the various aspects of a project, service, or facility to ensure that standards of quality are being met. QA is more than just testing the quality of a product, service or facility. It analyzes the quality to make sure it conforms to overall requirements and complies with established plans. It is important to realize that output quality is dependent on various factors which must be monitored. In fact, QA cannot absolutely guarantee the production of quality output, though it certainly makes this more likely.

5.5.1 Quality Assurance Process: The process of Quality Assurance is very rigorous. It requires proper planning, structured testing and correction in accordance with the result of measurement. The steps involves are:

1. Testing of output from the processes.
2. Planning for improvement.
3. Designing to meet basic requirements.
4. Manufacturing with improvements.
5. Reviewing performance after improvements.

As quality is determined by the intended users, clients or customers, not by society in general, it is not always true to assume 'expensive' for 'high quality'. Even goods with low prices can be considered quality items if they meet a consumer need. Quality assurance helps determine that the steps being used to provide the product or service of required quality are appropriate for the time and conditions. The working team has to comply with stated or implied requirements, implement new requirements and continuously improve the process for quality product that conforms to the changing consumers needs.

The most popular technique used for quality assurance is the *Plan*, *Do*, *Check*, and *Act (PDCA) cycle.*

1. **Plan:** Establish objectives and processes required to deliver the desired results,
2. **Do:** Implement the process developed,
3. **Check:** Monitor and evaluate the implemented process by testing the results against the predetermined objectives, and
4. **Act:** Apply actions necessary for improvement if the results require changes.

PDCA is an effective method for monitoring quality assurance because it analyzes existing conditions and methods used to provide the product or service to customers. The goal is to ensure that excellence is inherent in every component of the process. Quality assurance demands a degree of detail in order to be fully implemented at every step. *Planning*, for example, could include investigation into the quality of the raw materials used in manufacturing, the actual assembly, or the inspection processes. The *Checking* step could include customer feedback surveys, or other marketing vehicles to determine if customer needs are being exceeded and why they are not. *Acting* could mean a total revision in the manufacturing process in order to correct a technical or process flaw.

5.5.2 Accuracy of Quality Assurance: An extensive process of trial and error is involved in ensuring quality assurance. By the end of the trials one arrives at an acceptable process so that the output conforms to quality, reliability and other mandatory specification with regard to safety. The process of quality assurance being generally extensive, may delay production until all tests are conducted and acceptable level is reached. It is a systematic process of checking to see whether a product or service being developed meets specified requirements. Many companies have a separate department devoted to quality assurance. The quality assurance system aims at increasing customer confidence and a company's credibility, improving work processes and efficiency and enabling a company to perform better in comparison with its competitors.

5.5.3 Models and Standards: Many companies use ISO 9000 to ensure that their quality assurance system is in place and effective. Conformance to this standard is said to guarantee that a company delivers quality products and services. And to follow ISO 9000, a company's management team need to decide quality assurance policies and objectives.

ISO 17025 is an international standard that specifies the general requirements for the competence to carry out required tests and calibrations. There are 15 management requirements and 10 technical requirements. These requirements outline what a laboratory must do to become accredited. Management system refers to the structure of the organization for managing its processes and systems that transform inputs (including resources) into a product or service which meets the organization's objectives, such as satisfying the customer's quality requirements, complying with regulations, or meeting environmental objectives.

5.5.4 Quality Assurance for Software Development: The widely used QA models relating to the software development process in a business enterprise is the Capability Maturity Model Integration (CMMI) model. The CMMI maturity levels can be divided in to 5 steps, which a company can achieve by performing specific activities within the organization.

Despite success on the implementation of total quality, it did not find acceptance in many industries under the perceived notion that quality is costly. Such behaviour is common on the ground that top management lacks the proper understanding of quality, its effect on the product and services and the benefits the business can accrue. In fact, the top echelon continues to appreciate only the language of money and for them, profitability is the single most influencing criteria to implement any new idea or development. It is more relevant for business in small and medium sector and especially in developing countries like India. The traditional management seems obsessed with profit in the short-term and fails to appreciate the implicit cost burden of poor quality. Consequently, the industry suffers because of the prevailing perception that quality costs.

5.6 Economics of Quality

In the context of offering an unbiased view on the cost aspects to quality, Juran in 1950s discussed the concept of 'economics of quality'. It offers sufficient clarity on the cost implication of quality system implementation in a business organization. According to his theory, the cost involved in achieving quality could be divided into two groups: unavoidable cost (relating to inspection for quality control and prevention measures) and avoidable cost-cost of defects, rework and so on. He refers to the latter as 'gold in the mine' because there is scope for reduction of these costs of not 'doing the right things' which could have been avoided with a proper quality system in place. [8]

The objective of a cost analysis is twofold; first, the management should dispel their misconception that quality costs, and second, senior management may appreciate the implication of cost of quality. The ISO 9004-1987, 6.3 also endorses Juran's view that the quality costs can be broadly divided into costs associated with the provision of the service or product including those associated with external assurance: the cost of warranty and guaranty; and those relating to product quality improvement, appraisal for quality control. These costs and their relationship with quality are explained below in detail under the three distinct categories of unavoidable, avoidable and intangible costs.

5.6.1 Unavoidable Costs: The unavoidable costs could broadly be divided into two types—appraisal cost and prevention cost.

1. **Cost of Appraisal:** These costs are associated with the measurement essential for ascertaining that the product conforms to quality specification and meets the requirement of customer, the internal as well as the external. The related costs arise due to inspection and testing, external quality assessment and surveillance, quality audit, customer specified verification, appraisal of supplier and job workers.
2. **Cost of Prevention:** These costs are incurred for implementation of projects for improvement of processes with the objective to minimize the failure and defects. The actions are directed towards reducing failure costs and the actions include quality planning, developing quality systems and standards, tools techniques, measurement system and investment in instruments, vendor evaluation, inspection planning, training, motivational programmes and quality improvement.

5.6.2 Avoidable Costs: Certain costs arise in a manufacturing company when the products delivered to customers (the internal and external) suffer failures. These costs could be grouped as:

1. The internal failure costs are defined as the costs that arise within an organization due to non-conformance or defects at any stage of the production process. They cover:

- Re-work or re-process for conformance to standard.
- Re-testing including screening.
- Waste and scrap.
- Defect detection and analysis.

2. The external failure costs are the costs for which a company is liable after delivery of the product to customer due to guarantee and warranty. These cover mainly:

- Maintenance due to defects in functional requirement.
- Warranty returns, cost of claims.
- Direct extra cost for servicing due to failures in use.
- Cost of recall.
- Goodwill and company's image.

And all these costs illustrated above could be avoided by development and design of proper systems and processes for quality output and implementation of total quality certainly helps to achieve this objective.

5.6.3 Intangible Costs: The costs included in this category are difficult to quantify and thus difficult to measure. These aspects need consideration because they do more harm to the company. These are:

- Poor market reputation.
- Low morale of the employees.
- Loss of goodwill.

It also includes cost relating to all the opportunities foregone and expenses incurred due to 'not doing the right thing'. More importantly, it is to be noted that the costs of the second category could be eliminated or at least substantially reduced for the benefit of the company may benefit from it. A proper evaluation of the benefit from such implementation and costs involved with reference to investment made on quality improvement programme in an organization over a period of time would evidence its efficacy.

5.7 Total Quality Management

The total quality management (TQM) system promises to offer an integrative philosophy of management for continuously improving the quality of products and processes. It functions on the premise that achieving quality of the products and processes is the responsibility of everyone directly or indirectly engaged in the production process. In other words, it assumes involvement of all: management for their commitment to the programme and providing resources, workforce for active participation and diligent action, suppliers for quality inputs and the customers for positive feedback in order that the producers can meet and exceed customer expectations. Since the late 1980s, companies around the world have launched TQM programmes in an attempt to retain or regain market position with customer satisfaction in the face of increasing competition in this era of globalization.

TQM today has become a buzzword in industry circles. It however offers varied connotations. Huge volume of quality literature including the writings of distinguished experts who pioneered the movement, developed concepts and systems conveys different approaches: Deming's PDCA cycle, Juran's Trilogy, Ishikawa's Kaizen, Crosby's 'right first time' and many more added to the management vocabulary. [9]

The objective however remains uniquely focused—TQM integrates fundamental management techniques, exacts improvement efforts and employs quality tools under a disciplined approach for continual improvement. [10] The activities ultimately aim at attaining increased customer/user satisfaction. Dean and Bowen (1994) suggest that 'the key principles of TQM are customer focus, continuous improvement and teamwork. And these principles are deployed through a series of scientifically designed tools and techniques'.

5.7.1 Pre-requisite: The implementation necessitates participation of all departments to approach quality with an open mind. Success would be inevitable if the top management could lead the quality improvement initiative. There is thus need for sincere effort to address some common deficiencies that have been ignored or have escaped attention. The most important amongst these are:

1. Marketing should have a system of collecting consumer feed back on the company's product and reporting to management periodically.
2. The feedback from the user/customer should form the basis for design review or redesign.
3. The requirements of customer are technically defined by way of product specifications and must be incorporated in the design for quality output.
4. Drawings, standards and other relevant documents are prepared for manufacturing, measurement and control.
5. Inspections are carried out not only on components but also on materials bought in or otherwise as per laid down standards and procedure for conformance to the specifications. This is the responsibility of the QA/QC department.
6. A company should establish a system of dealing complaints received from the customers to their satisfaction.
7. Consistent data recording, assessment and documentation should be part of the established procedure.
8. Proper communication to all concerned regarding changes, if any proposed by management must be notified.
9. Top management must take leadership role for continuous improvement, ensure employees participation and involvement, provides enabling working environment in order to achieve quality culture in the organization.

5.7.2 The Principle: In practice, total quality is considered to have three main components: quality control, quality assurance of products and services for consistency in quality and quality improvement to take care of the ever changing customer needs and preferences. It involves application of measures for attaining quality in every activity of the business organisation and is characterised by the good practice of management principles and techniques. The emphasis is not only on product/service quality, but also the means to achieve it and improve upon.

It is total, companywide because it entails commitment of the senior management for providing leadership and motivation to ensure involvement of all employees. The principles that can be used by upper management to guide their action towards improved performance cover:

1. Management leadership.
2. System approach.
3. Customer focus.
4. Continual improvement.
5. Involvement of people through empowerment.
6. Decision-making based on facts.
7. Mutually beneficial supplier-customer relationships.

The British Quality Association offers three alternate approaches:

1. The first deals with qualitative characteristics involving themes such as customer satisfaction achieved through a culture of excellence ensuring participation of employees, team work focusing on 'imaginative concept for continuously improving the quality of goods and services delivered through the participation of all levels and function' (Evans and Lindsay, 1993:28).
2. Second puts priority on production aspects such as setting standards of performance, measurement with statistical procedures to assess quality. It involves a 'set of techniques and procedures used to reduce or eliminate variation in a production process, or service delivery system in order to improve efficiency, reliability and quality' (Steingard and Fitzgibbons, 1993).
3. While the first is viewed as a soft approach and second 'hard', the third aims at attaining quality prudently combining the important aspects from both, i.e. involvement of all employees for achieving organizational

goal ('soft' approach) and the scientific evaluation for control ('hard' approach).

5.7.3 Implementation: Yahagi (1992) lists 12 factors that relate to excellent quality management: corporate history, corporate climate, strategic alliances, channels, management cycle, environment, management targets, business structure, management resources, management design, management functions and management performance. He identifies a set of six of these as critical to the success of an organization, which are:

1. Corporate climate—enabling business environment and quality culture.
2. Management cycle—planning, organizing, implementing and controlling.
3. Business structure—preferred market segment, market leadership.
4. Management resources—factors of production.
5. Management design—developing systems for all functions in the organization.
6. Management performance—market share, stability, growth and profit.

One of the most systematic frameworks for understanding and implementing TQM is Malcolm Baldrige National Quality Award criteria. A Baldrige examiner [11] with his long experience in evaluating applications for award identifies four 'cross-cutting themes' that companies implementing quality improvement programmes need to develop for achieving outstanding product quality:

1. Understanding of 'processes',
2. Effective management by fact,
3. To set clear priorities, and
4. Primary focus on the workforce (leaving out the role of management and technical personnel).

The management provides leadership and framework for vision, objective, strategy, policy, procedure and practices to ensure better performance. Some experts believe that implementation of total quality with ultimate aim of establishing quality culture is assuming importance and the critical factors that need to be reckoned with include:

1. Organizing for quality that aims at excellence through development of organizational structure and systems for quality management and improvement.
2. Motivation of employees that is influenced by the internal and external environment in addition to management attitude towards human relation and empowerment of people involved.
3. Product/service standards and measurements that are often imposed by government for safety and industry is bound to comply with them.
4. Culture and Values that generally affect the acceptance of quality philosophy and goals of quality.

These are considered essential elements for success. The total quality measures aim at improving not only the quality of product and services but establishing quality organization and quality culture.

While some argue to the contrary that high tides of TQM has receded, the industry today accepts its effectiveness. [12] Its impact on business performance has been phenomenal. [13] It would continue to play a very critical role for the growth of industry.

5.8 Quality Culture

A quality culture 'consists of values, traditions, procedures and expectations that promote quality' (Goetsch and Davis, 1994:122). The important elements of an ideal quality culture in a business enterprise would include:

1. Sincere desire to work efficiently for achieving goal.
2. Teamwork approach to work.
3. Ease and friendly work environment.
4. Quick response to address customers' grievances.
5. Democratic and/or, cooperative management style.
6. Harmonious relationship among employees.

7. Open communication.

It is often noticed that many organizations do an excellent job of committing to total quality, provide resources, training for empowerment of employees, only to have their effort fall flat. It is perhaps due to inertia inherent to the system or people resist change as a natural human instinct. Juran (1989) points out that 'all large organizations exhibit some of the features of a biological organism. The organism senses the intrusion of the alien and mobilizes to reject it'. It is, therefore, a lesson for the management to judiciously initiate steps for activating cultural changes necessary to establish a quality organization in the overall social frame with full knowledge and awareness of their cultural background and motivating them to change the attitude so that the change happens.

A business organization, in true sense being a miniature society would reflect the culture of the society in which it operates. The culture is the integration social traditions, value systems followed over a long period of time. A firm similarly develops its own systems and tradition and the practice becomes a way of life for its members. Many factors contribute to the development of an organizational culture: the value system including ethics followed by the top management to working level often reflects in its business practice—how the managers treat the employees, how the employees take interest in the activities for accomplishing set goals, how they respond to the customers' problem, how they interact among themselves and level of harmony in the business environment.

It is natural that the values we respect guide our behaviour, as it is deeply ingrained forming the vary core of our character. Knowledge and skills are important, but these alone do not guarantee results. It is because the employees as individuals in an organization would apply the knowledge and skills to what they value, what they believe in, what they feel important. Their attitude influences their performance and drive for excellence. Expectations too are important determinant to organizational culture: what management expects from employees and what the employees in turn expect from the management.

Improvement in essence is the change for the better. Continuous improvement thus would mean continuous change and for achieving it, management must facilitate change as a change agent through development of change promoting strategies. The strategies require an advocacy paradigm, proper planning and action with effective deployment of tools and techniques. Some important steps for initiating change are explained below:

1. **Identify Attitude and Behaviour of Employees:** Generally, people want status quo, contented in the comfort zone. Some by instinct are adventurous- like to take risk, challenge and experiment with new ideas. These people are to be identified in the organization to act as agents of change. Tools like Force Field Analysis and Theory of Constraint could be usefully deployed.

   And those who resist change should be given opportunity to state their cases. Managers must listen to their concerns, which may be uncertainty, their unfounded fear, burden of more work or an emotional response (shock and denial). Doubts in their minds should be removed by providing adequate information on past achievement, potential gains from change. Managers should try to involve the potential resistors during planning to implementation so that they develop a sense of ownership.
2. **Create a Positive Environment:** Change cannot occur in a hostile environment. The managers should display patience, respect others views, appreciate their concerns, treat them with trust, dignity for better relationship. Appropriate management style, openness in communication will ensure total involvement. It is to be noted that moving to total quality system takes time. It is not instant. An enabling environment helps accelerate the process.
3. **Move Slowly, Steadily and Be Flexible:** Predictability is

an important factor for successful implementation. The result of change initiatives being unpredictable, it is advisable to move slowly at first giving scope to resistors to evaluate the benefits. Any doubts raised must be responded quickly and positively. Flexibility is another attribute for success.

4. **Adopt Pro-active Approach:** The managers and supervisors involved should have an open mind to accept new ideas. Suggestions from any quarters must be accepted, analyzed and applied if considered useful to the organization. Rather, there should be a system of inviting suggestion for improvement including rewards for practical and useful ones.
5. **Continuously Improve Programme for Change:** The organizational change requirement is dynamic. The management must respond to the changing need professionally and quickly in consultation with all concerned. The process involved is an emotional transition. It consists of some or all of the steps-shock, denial, realization, acceptance, rebuilding, understanding and recovery. And these must be addressed properly.

The employee at all levels should also be aware of the fact that quality culture is a sincere attempt for continuous improvement in order to accomplish the goal of the business: meeting and exceeding customers' expectations.

End Notes

1. Shewhart, W. A. '*Economic Control of Quality of Manufactured Product*' Van Nostrand, New York, 1931.
2. Measurement tells us where we are and where we are going.
3. Juran (1993).
4. Rampey, J. And H. Roberts 'Perspectives in Total Quality' Proceedings of Total Quality Forum IV, Cincinnati, November, 1992.
5. To Japanese quality expert, Dr. Noriaki Kano, 'Quality is too important to be left to inspectors.' He emphasized the need for worker self-inspection.
6. Lindsay, William M. and Joseph A. Petrick 'Total Quality and

Organization Development' St. Lucie Press, 1997: 20-36.

7. By 1970s, the Japanese cars regularly top the J. D. Power customer satisfaction rating.
8. The cost of poor quality to be valued in terms of money for the effort, material, resource, time, risks, goodwill including opportunities lost.
9. Hackman and Wageman in their article '*Total Quality Management: empirical, conceptual and practical issues*' examine to what extent TQM philosophy is distinct from other organizational improvement strategies.
10. Oakland in '*Total Quality Management: The Route to Improving Performance*' sums up, 'TQM is based on the premise that all activities in a firm contribute to quality'.
11. Easton, George S. '*Total Quality Management: A Baldrige Examiner's Perspective*' California Management Review, Spring, 1993:32-48.
12. Hill (1995) points out that the commonly made distinction between efficiency and effectiveness has been resolved with TQM with its dual focus: 'doing things right' and 'doing right things'.
13. Jacob, Rahul in '*TQM: More than a Dying Fad*' writes, 'But make no mistakes: thoughtfully applied and modified total quality principles still represent a sound way to run a company'(October 1993:66).

6

Transiting to Total Quality

In theory, total quality offers a number of measures for the improvement of performance of a business organization and the scope for success enhances with the commitment of top management for providing leadership. Wilkinson et al. (1998) in this context confirm that, 'quality is a management leadership issue: the way management thinks, behaves and structures systems which is pivotal to success. In fact, the management is charged with ultimate responsibility for quality because 85 percent failures are reckoned to be the fault of inadequate management system'. Today's market dynamics, fast pace technological development and innovations too demand that the management must adopt, adapt, change attitude and look ahead professionally with a clear vision to bring about transformation for achieving desired result.

Lindsay and Petrick (1997) 'hold a strong belief, along with countless theorists, practicing managers and consultants that these new challenges can most effectively be tackled within the context of a TQM philosophy.' The management responsibility thus relates to pursuing total quality system for establishing a quality organization and quality culture. And keeping in view that quality management has a strong positive co-relation with organizational transformation, total quality programmes are often introduced as a part of wider change initiative.

Juran, however, considers organizational change a 'clash between cultures' [1] and the cultures refer to the existing day-to-day activity *vis-à-vis* the quality culture that is envisaged. 'Effecting such a change would primarily depend on the management leadership for developing a quality policy, planning and strategy for implementation' he adds.

6.1 Management Leadership

Leadership, in a generic sense, could be described as the 'process of social influence in which one person can enlist the aid and support of others in accomplishing a common task'. [2] In the context of industry and business, 'effective leadership is the ability to successfully integrate available resources within the internal and external environment and optimally utilize for attaining organizational or societal goals.' The management must appreciate that quality is not an assignable task and therefore the system must be rooted and institutionalized in every process. It must be everyone's responsibility. [3] The managers as leaders must be 'capable of inspiring others for achieving defined objectives set by the organization. The leaders assigned the responsibility for accomplishing the goals have to be quality zealots. [4]

And for developing a good leadership, as it has been experienced, not only technical or managerial acumen, but a deep perspective on human behaviour to steer through the transition are essential. Some general recommendation would include:

1. It is necessary to take care of the basics. Introducing new systems and technologies when people don't have the fundamental skills to work in the new system is a prescription for disaster.
2. Basic concepts like 'what is quality?', should relate easily to everyone's job. It should be simple and practical.
3. Systems for technical and social changes must proceed on parallel path in order that they are synergetic. People are more receptive to new ways of management and working together when the systems are changing.
4. Learning should from a part of routine in the organization. Management should learn with open mind from a variety of industries, even those that are not doing so well, as it is commonly believed. It broadens the horizon and the scope for better quality management decisions: procurement policy, the sales process, hiring and promotion, training

and every other aspect of the business. They all influence customer satisfaction.

5. It is not prudent to rely fully on the advice of famous experts to make all decisions in the company. None of them has a complete answer, but at the same time, they all have something worthwhile to say. Learning from them and becoming one's own guide is pragmatic.
6. There is need to concentrate on value driven approach, for quality is an ethic and more important than financial return. When it is held as a higher standard, there is more buy-in from employees. The financial return may not reflect the higher customer satisfaction including market image and goodwill as cost reduction, but it pays in the long-run.

In fact, quality begins with leadership and developing effective leadership traits begins with an appreciation of the options available [5] and management assuming responsibility is an essential prerequisite for implementing total quality. Their commitments to the project, understanding of the basic tenets and adapting to change are of paramount importance.

6.2 Commitment of Senior Management

Successful people in business are hailed as visionary leaders. A careful examination of their personal traits would evidence that they are individuals holding firmly to a simple set of commitments, usually grounded in beliefs such as offering 'the best product for the value of money' or 'the highest possible customer satisfaction'. It is their strength, religiously following definite principles that leads to the business success. 'Their basic philosophy, spirit and drive have far more to do with achievements than do financial or economic resources, organizational structure, or modern management practices. All these things weigh heavily in success, but they are transcended by how strongly the people in the organization believe in its basic precepts and how faithfully they carry them out. [6]

The most basic of these is a commitment to a set of values, principles or beliefs. The underlying principles define both the organization's uniqueness and the fundamental direction in which it wants to proceed. This first commitment leads to a common vision and purpose for the organization as a whole. A positive commitment to self determination for pursuing a set of principles serves as a strong foundation to effectively provide direction for accomplishing organizational goal.

It is the combination of both supporting and sharing behaviour that makes up the practice of commitment. A strong and healthy organization also shows its commitment to the people. When management supports its employees, they are willing and encouraged to achieve intended results. When these results support customer needs and expectations, customers will support the organization in their business.

Juran concludes, 'to my knowledge, no company has attained world class quality without upper management leadership.' Senior managers are the systems gatekeepers. Once they open the gates to change, the transition begins. Their commitment is thus a primary requirement. It is however seen in real life that most people try to tiptoe around to continue with the existing established practice, for 'change is such a difficult thing'. It is, however, essential for the management to change attitude and style of functioning as these are essential components of leadership for organizational transformation. And full awareness of what is expected, how to proceed are key to effective leadership.

6.3 Understanding Business

Deming's views are succinct, 'It is not enough that top management commits itself for life to quality and productivity. They must know what it is that they are committed to-that is, what they must do. These obligations cannot be delegated. Support is not enough; action is required.' It is also a very common experience that a company is successful when the senior management understands its job. Understanding is joyous. [7] It is because, we are intelligent species and the use of our intelligence quite properly gives us pleasure. In this respect the brain is like muscle. When it is in use we feel very good.

Dumas make a very important point, 'no organization-wide system should be adopted until management understands its role to lead by example and creates quality ethic that is supported by its own systems and daily behaviour'. [8] The better one understands the subject matter, the more one is able to weave past experiences (context) into new knowledge by absorbing, doing, interacting. It will naturally reflect in the style of functioning.

6.4 Management Style

Deming advocates a 'transformation of the management style' [9] in '*Out of Crisis*' for a seamless transition to a successful quality organization. Though he said this in the context of American managers, the statement enjoys universal validity. Global competition is quickly making the old management model obsolete. The new market environment demands a paradigm shift in management approach from the traditional model that emphasizes more on increasing production, reducing cost for profit to the new model that focuses on meeting the customers' needs and preferences. It is thus imperative for the managers to move away from the traditional autocratic style of functioning to more open participative style.

Table 6.1 offers a comparison of the important parameters that are set to change in the new model.

The practicing managers come across situations where these concepts are re-interpreted by managers who are obsessed with short-term targets and reluctant to change their management style; give up power and accept a more proactive role, be a facilitator rather than commander in an army. A total quality orientation for managing organizational change redefines line managerial role and accords new responsibilities to the supervisory management function. The role of latter now includes inputs to strategic plans and continual development of the organization's systems and processes. The goal of these changes is to increase customer satisfaction now and in the future (Lindsay and Petrick, 1997:3). But in order to bring about effective change for establishing total quality organization, intervention of top management is required with the clear understanding why changes are required.

Table 6.1: Change in Management Perspective

Parameter	Traditional Model	New Model
Objective	Profit through Cost Reduction	Customer Satisfaction
Organization Structure	Vertical	Horizontal
Leadership Style	Autocratic	Cooperative
Structure	Self-Sufficient	Interdependent
Market	Domestic	Global
Approach To Work	Individual Performance	System Efficiency
Quality Culture	Imposed	Motivated

6.5 Establishing Quality Culture

Technically, introduction of total quality system in an organization comprises application of quality concepts, relevant tools and techniques. The process entails a paradigm shift from the traditional to new professional approach. Some consider that transformational change works best when an enterprise faces a crisis and changes are readily accepted in order to survive. Even in Japan, for example, Carlos Ghosn led a transformational change at Nissan Motor Company which was in a financial and operational crisis. Yet another school considers the transformation has to be dramatic with quality leadership and pragmatic management approach.

On the other hand, a contrary view prevails with equal emphasis that changes need to be gradual for long-term gains in accordance with the principles of *Kaizen*. It is easier and often more effective to work within the existing cultural boundaries and make small improvements than to make sudden and major transformational changes. Use of *Kaizen* in Japan has been a path breaking experience for its industrial and economic strength. And whatever may be the method adopted, an important lesson: improvements that change the culture take longer as they have to overcome greater resistance to change.

From a practitioner's point, labels are not important. The relevant aspects are to be selected for implementation and other elements discarded. In this context, Cole (1993) suggests that the best firms should do is to incorporate each of the good elements in the system to bring about organizational transformation.

Managing total quality thus is viewed as a major and long-term challenge for organization, with far reaching implications for management style and organizational culture (Wilkinson *et al.* 1998:177). It attempts to orient the business consumer-driven, continuous improvement and top management providing leadership for pursuing organizational goal.

6.6 Customer Orientation

Quality means meeting customers' needs and preferences. While traditionally, conformance to quality has been the focus of the production process, it remains inadequate unless the product or service delivered meets or exceeds customer expectation. And in order to achieve this goal, quality must be a way of life in the organization and permeate quality culture in every sphere of activity of the enterprise. Tuckman (1995), concludes that 'the central feature of total quality is the idea of cultural change grafted into earlier quality management theory and practice. Total quality is the key element of workplace transformation.

Gabor's account of Deming's influence to provide customer service is an interesting example of customer orientation. It relates to the paint process developed at Ford in

1958 to deal with rust problem. While the finance department argued that rusting occurred outside the warranty period and the company would not be responsible to bear additional expenditure to prevent it, the spirit of quality orientation prevailed and rust free paint was provided. Such an effort was necessary in keeping with customer satisfaction, long-term interest of gaining market image and goodwill.

This presents orientation towards external customers. There are also internal customers within the organization: the operator whose work follows that of another operator is a customer and the employee whose work precedes another is a supplier. Thus customers are the people who receive the work and only they can determine what quality is, only they can tell what they want and how they want. A quality organization recognizes both external and internal customers, those who purchase for using product or service and fellow employees whose work depends on the work that precedes them respectively (Gabor, 1990:97).

A customer, whether external or internal, depends on the supplier for quality product and for an internal customer the supplier-customer relationship is also critical due to dependency. For example, an assembly line worker gets parts and components from others work stations who are the supplier and their quality would affect the final product. Working in collaboration with the customers to access their needs is of prime importance to the producer. That's why a popular slogan in quality movement is 'quality begins with the customer' (Scholtes, 1992:2).

Merli (1990) also points out that customer defines quality of a product or service, and therefore:

1. The customer must be organization's top priority. The organization's survival depends on them.
2. A reliable customer is the one who buys the product repeatedly from same organization. It confirms that he is satisfied with the quality. Therefore, customer satisfaction is essential.

3. Satisfaction to be ensured with quality of product or service offered and continuous improvement is the only way to keep customers satisfied and loyal, for quality that a customer wants is not static.

The key to establishing a customer orientation thus should begin with interacting customers and sincerely incorporating their requirement into the product features that satisfy their requirement. This is the first step towards achieving the objective.

6.7 Identifying Customer Needs

Scholtes recommends a six-step strategy for data collection by interaction and it focuses on to:

1. Decide information to be collected.
2. Develop an information gathering plan.
3. Gather information (unedited, as conveyed by customers is preferred).
4. Analyze the information carefully and objectively.
5. Check the validity of the conclusion (customers may help).
6. Take action for incorporating the required characteristics in the product-either by product modification or design/redesign for development.

Application of QFD technique is an ideal strategy. It helps establishing an operational structure for the system of integrating quality in the product from the initial stage of manufacturing and this is essentially 'customer focus'.

6.8 Customer Focus Organization

The companies that have successfully established customer focus present a set of characteristics common to them and these include:

1. Clear vision, top management commitment and allocation of resource.
2. Reaching out to customers and communicating with them.
3. Use of customer information in product development.
4. Continuous improvement with application of appropriate

techniques such as QFD, Six Sigma etc.
5. Empowering people with training.
6. Enlisting their involvement through management leadership.
7. Willingness to find and eliminate customers' problem [10] for enhancing their satisfaction.

In fact, customer satisfaction is regarded as the only relevant objective for ensuring stable and continuously increasing business (Merli, 1990:84).

6.9 Continuous Improvement

An essential element of managing total quality is continuous improvement of product, process and people. The manufacturers and service providers need to accept the fact that customer needs are not static. It keeps on changing. A special product feature may be considered innovative today, but it becomes regular in a few days and out of fashion sometime later. Sweeping technological advancement and innovations are facilitating faster new development. Improvement of features in the existing product and making it free from defects is very important. A quality organization must aim at achieving both; implementing continuous improvement and introducing innovative features that suits the specific need. Companies that are just maintaining the status quo in such key areas as quality, new product development, the adoption of new technologies and process performance are like a runner who is sitting still in a race. Competing in global marketplace is like competing in the Olympic.(Goetsch and Davis, 1994:433).

6.10 Role of Management

Management should provide the necessary leadership for introducing a system for continuous improvement. Commitment of senior management is essential. It is not enough to establish policies, create awareness and then leave all these to subordinates. That has been tried, over and over again, with disappointing results [11] (Juran, 1989:72).

It must be kept in mind that solving isolated problem is not continuous improvement. The management should objectively decide the vision of the company, clearly define quality improvement goals, provides resources required to accomplish objectives, strategize for the short-term and long-term, monitor progress and communicate with all employees.

The important activities crucial to continuous improvement would include the following:

1. **Effecting Permanent Solution:** A problem may be small or big. It is to be taken seriously for immediate identification of causes and finding permanent solution. The scientific approach to look for root causes include:
    - Collection of meaningful data.
    - Analysis using quality tools to find root causes of the problem.
    - Developing appropriate solutions.
    - Action for rectification to bring the process under control.
2. **Maintaining Communication:** Communication plays a very critical role in employee's participation and involvement. A well informed worker tends to appreciate the management initiative for change and its consequences. Proper communication explaining the objective of the actions being taken along with expected results is a necessity, lest the employee should think in isolation that consequent to restructuring, there may be downsizing and job loss.

    In the context of enlisting employee's involvement sharing information before, during and after programme implementation is necessary. Open communication has paramount effect on the motivational propensity that results in worker's commitment to work. Cameron (1994), argues that 'The most productive total quality firms are those whose employees 'personalize' quality practices in their work'.

3. **Documenting Development:** Available documents on positive outcomes provide details of analysis and effect of improvement. It serves as a guide for all.
4. **Monitoring Progress:** It is very important for the management to know the result of action taken. As there is possibility that the system parameters often change, continuous improvement and measurement are the only way to ensure that the process are stable and output conforms to specification.

6.11 Improvement Plan

Quality improvement does not just happen. It requires consorted effort, structured programme for implementation in order to achieve quality objective. It should begin with selection of a project, based on Pareto principle. [12] And the next step is organizing for improvement by implementation of the selected project through formation of the lead team.

It is also to be appreciated that 'one-size-fit-all' method for improving process is rather difficult as processes vary widely and demand specific solution set. [13] A standard strategy for process improvement which can be used as a baseline is presented:

1. Understand the process—the project team assigned to improve the project should clearly understand the process. Describing the process with a flow chart of the process sequence helps to understand better.
2. Identify special causes of variation—the process needs to be analyzed and root causes are identified using the quality tools and techniques like fishbone diagram, the CEDAC, control charts.
3. Eliminate process variation—rectification of the process errors eliminates the variation and the process is under control and we get quality output from the process in stable state.
4. Streamline the process—is to take slack out of the process, for example eliminating unnecessary steps, reducing cycle

time. It is an important step in process improvement.

5. Monitor Progress and Establish Continuous Improvement—improvement in any related area of activity is welcome. It can be achieved through active participation and a well designed programme of experimentation.

Identification of customers, collecting information from them, analyzing the information and taking required action-ensuring the products meet their standard, monitoring for conformance, offering after sales service are components of continuous improvement.

For the implementation of total quality and especially the continuous improvement in a business organization, there is need for a pragmatic approach for management practice to shift from traditional emphasis on price, quantity and delivery to application of quality approach for continuous development. The employees involved in operation may need training on quality initiatives, procedure and practices including basic knowledge of quality tools and the modern techniques for effecting improvement, which include:

- Kaizen;
- Theory of constraint;
- Cause-and-effect diagram with the addition of cards (CEDAC);
- Quality function deployment (QFD);
- Benchmarking;
- Statistical process control (SPC);
- Just-in-time (JIT) manufacturing; and
- Six Sigma.

Elaborating the benefits of continuous improvement Deming notes that, 'with each improvement, processes and systems run better and better. Productivity increases as waste goes down. Customers get better products, which ultimately increases market share and provides better return on investment' (quoted in Scholtes, 1992:1).

Success of the implementation of total quality however would depend to a large extent on the attitude of management.

Limited management outlook—short-term focus on profit and dividend, very little attention to customer needs and preferences, equating high price with good quality and above all authoritarian style must change for creating quality environment in the organization to effectively cope with the dynamic market environment. Understanding the 14 points [Deming's philosophy for quality system application] can shape a new attitude toward work and the work environment that will foster continuous improvement (Scholtes, 1992:2).

6.12 Focus on Product, Process and People

In recent times some themes that have assumed more significance for establishing a quality organization, are systems approach, management leadership and management commitment. Experience however suggests that a holistic approach to quality is imperative in order to bring about transformation. Thus, product, process and people are considered together rather than independent factors in quality management.

6.12.1 Product: A product is defined as a thing 'produced by labour or effort' or the 'result of an act or a process'. [14] In marketing, a product is anything that can be offered to consumers for satisfying some of their needs. In general, product may refer to a single item or unit, a group of equivalent products, a grouping of goods or services as per the industrial classification for the goods or services.

The manufacturer and consumers have their own perspective on the quality of a product. The manufacturers' concern primarily relates to the design, engineering, and production processes involved in manufacturing a product. Quality is measured by the degree of conformance to predetermined specifications and standards and deviations from the standard can lead to poor quality and low reliability. Since a firm's objective is to improve product quality, its effort should focus on:

1. Understanding customer needs.

2. Analyzing feedback for corrective action.
3. Designing within process capabilities.
4. Producing items to specified standards.
5. Measuring critical parameters for control.
6. Establishing processes for quality output.

In addition, it aims at eliminating defects at components and subsystems stage such that the final product conforms to specification. To consumers, a high-quality product is one that well satisfies the functional requirement; it is reliable and safe for use in addition to its availability and reasonable price. Product quality is achieved by providing a number of features and characteristics that contribute to its ability to meet stated and implied functions. As consumers are becoming more and more conscious of the cost and quality of products and services, firms have begun to focus on achieving product quality at minimum cost. The present trend seems obvious that market is largely driven by consumer concerns and preferences. This necessitates coordination and integration of almost all the departments in a manufacturing organization since they directly or indirectly contribute to quality of output.

6.12.2 Process: A process converts or transforms inputs to create an output. It is defined as a sequence of interdependent and linked procedures which, at every stage consume one or more resources (man, machine, money, time and energy) for the conversion of inputs (material, data, components) into designed output. The output may be offered in marketplace for external customer or may serve as inputs for the next stage of operation within the company (internal customer) until the final product is made. This is essentially a production process in a manufacturing company.

The process approach is one of the 'Eight principles of Quality management'. It forms the basis of ISO 9001:2008. Thareja writes about the mechanism and benefits: 'The process (proficiency) may be limited in words, but not in its applicability. While it fulfils the criteria of all-round gains, in terms of the competencies augmented by the participants; the organization seeks newer directions to the business success, the individual brand image of both the people and the organization, in turn, goes up. The competencies which were hitherto rated as being smaller are better recognized and now acclaimed to be more potent and fruitful.'

Scientifically, an organization could be considered as a collection of interrelated processes. In other words, the activities within an organization can be broken into basic tasks or processes-the input, production process to output are linked in a series or 'quality chain' to form the organization and each department in the chain has to align its action and contribute in coeval with the ultimate organizational goal. And in order to manage process integration, a variety of process assessment tools, such as process mapping, data modelling are generally used. Process design also involves people integrating people with the process is an opportunity for the management for ensuring better performance.

6.12.3 People: Transiting to a total quality organization being essentially a cultural change, it involves people the most. It entails changing people's beliefs and attitudes which is one of the most difficult tasks facing management, who must develop their own powers and skills of motivation and persuasion (Dale and Cooper, 1992:20). There is, therefore, need to approach quality from a deeper humanistic perspective and considerable thought needs to be given to managing people, for logic can hardly change emotion and behaviour.

Behavioural scientists believe that attempting to motivate people to change on logical grounds and arguments is a futile exercise. It is perception that controls emotion and emotion controls behaviour. Thus, perception is the key and in order to change the employees' perception, the management should demonstrate by action, set example, managers assume the role of facilitator and coordinator and work together for integrating individual effort towards organizational goal.

Total quality performance management also includes treatment of quantum quality issues that contribute immensely to 'achieving breakthroughs in customer delight through increased personal motivation and commitment to quality'. [15] Employees sincerely participate in defining quality not only with the application of control charts and controlling statistical process variation, but as a sense of pride in craftsmanship and satisfaction in delighting customers. In order to sustain the involvement of employees, the work culture must support self-managed learning, respect personal and organizational integrity, individual creativity, encourage adaptation of emerging development for change. [16] Quality management literature too suggests that 'employees are to be won over, not by compulsion but by leadership, communication, training and recognition'. [17]

Structured programmes for cultural change, tailored to suit the specific need of a company are designed by experts aiming to break the 'mind-sets', win 'hearts and minds' that would ultimately change attitudes and values to be more supportive of strategic objectives. Business organizations must appreciate that 'a strong culture is a system of informal rules that spell out how people are to behave most of the time, it enables people to feel better about what they do, so they are more likely to work harder' (Deal and Kennedy, 1982:15).

An organization cannot afford to underestimate the people factor, such as culture, in selecting a quality improvement approach. Management need to appreciate that improvement (change) takes time to implement, gain acceptance and stabilize as accepted practice. Improvement must allow pauses between implementing new changes so that the change is stabilized and assessed as a real improvement, before the next improvement is made (hence continual improvement). And to effect planned change for accomplishing the goal of a desired future, concerted efforts are necessary on a wide spectrum of areas and systems that contribute to increasing productivity and organizational efficiency. Most critical amongst these are employees at all levels who must be empowered with education and training.

6.13 Empowerment of Employees for Involvement

Involvement and empowerment have distinct meaning in total quality approach, sometime however it is used interchangeably creating scope for misrepresentation especially by detractors. Involvement is active participation and the basis for involving employees is twofold: first, by bringing more minds, more ideas of people who are closest to the work, having firsthand experience in order to increase the likelihood of a good decision, a better plan and more effective way of implementing improvement and second, promoting ownership of decisions by people who are responsible to implement them.

Empowerment would simply mean to provide opportunity in such a way that the employees are trained to be fully aware of the process, the operations they perform. They are encouraged to have a say, make decisions for improvement of product and process, though within specified parameters. They can effectively contribute only when they know the causes and effect of different actions and practices. For example, a machine operator can and should be encouraged to reduce initial setup time by his experience with innovative practice but not authorised to unilaterally select a vendor.

And meaningful involvement occurs when the employees are fully aware of their work, technical parameters that govern the process and limitations. Scholtes (1992) asserts that, 'all employees must understand their job and their role in the company; and how these roles change as quality improves. Such understanding goes beyond the instructions given in manuals or job descriptions. Employees need to know where their work fits into the larger context: how their work is influenced by workers who precede them and how their work influences workers who follow. They must learn new skills for improving work.'

6.13.1 Management's Role: Commitment, leadership and facilitation are essential elements of management for successful implementation of programme enlisting employees' involvement.

The leadership role entails a participatory style with a judicious balance of task-orientation and people-orientation and above all creating supportive environment that would foster creativity and innovation. Management ought to be sincere in their effort by: (a) removing barriers, i.e. open to interact with employees at all levels, (b) developing an open culture—open to new ideas, evaluating objectively and implementing in the overall interest of the organization, and (c) accepting criticism with humility. The only preconditions are that employees know what is expected of them, know that organization cares for them, possesses the resources to do their job and know they have authority to act (Townsend and Gebhardt, 1992:11).

The following systems may be introduced for increasing employees' participation:

1. Suggestion system for improvement: this offers an opportunity to all, particularly those who think about improvement to suggest for the benefit of the organization. Every organization needs a well defined system for accepting suggestion, analyzing and adapting, if considered useful in the best interest of the organization.
2. Brainstorming session for finding solution to problems: it is generally convened by the manager to get ideas that may help find better solution. The group of operators, supervisor working have potential to think.
3. Quality Circle: a group comprising volunteers from the work environment regularly meet, before, during or after working hours, to discuss and recommend the management about development required. The team leader may work as facilitator.
4. Reward for good work: it creates a healthy competition among peers and nurtures creativity.

6.13.2 Education and Training: The experts, consultants and practicing managers tend to agree that 'the employees of a company to be happy in their work, essentially three things are needed: they must be fit for it, they must not do too much of it and they must have a sense of success in it. [18] And to ensure that they are fit candidates, the company must recruit people with right aptitude, train them for the specific job assignment and provide enabling work environment. This could be achieved by a system of education and training activities designed for enhancing an individual's work related knowledge, skill, understanding in keeping with the development of tools, techniques, technology and innovations.

Training of employees at all levels therefore should be a regular activity in any organization. It is seen that trained and well informed workers and managers are better motivated than the untrained. It is essential component for launching total quality programme. The programme however has to be properly planned and structured, clearly defining the training requirement to bridge the deficiencies: the gap between: (a) what knowledge, skill and attitude the employees need to have to be best-in-class, and (b) the knowledge, skill and attitude the employees possess.

Shewhart recognized the need and advocated that the managers should regularly discuss with the workers on the operational requirement with operators, inspectors and supervisors alike. His fond rhetoric, 'how can an operator carry out his job tasks if he does not understand what the job is?' This is possible only through education and training, well structured for the specific product and process. [19] The knowledge gained would benefit not only the individuals but also the organization. The workers including the managers are motivated to focus on the organizational goal, actively participate in implementing continuous improvement for excellence and work as a team with sincerity and devotion. Workers put on their best efforts, when they are empowered they are in complete awareness of the systems, procedures and the implications there of. To sum up, the training should be designed in such a way that:

1. The worker knows what he is supposed to do.

2. The worker knows the result of his work.
3. The worker is equipped with knowledge to influence the result. [20]

It is in this context important to note the finding of a study; 'the companies that practice total quality, the median number of hours devoted to quality training (per employee/month) was 20, with a larger commitment in corporations just launching their total quality efforts'. [21]

6.13.3 Benefits: The employees' involvement and participation benefit the organization in many ways and some of the important ones are:

1. Participation generally results in better decisions and successful implementation, for people are more likely to implement decisions they have made themselves. It satisfies the basic human instinct, as one always thinks, 'wouldn't it be better to be a part of deciding what changes will be made rather than having to adjust to them'.
2. Participation improves communication and cooperation. It increases loyalty and identification with the organization.
3. It enhances people's sense of power and dignity. It frequently results in goal setting. Participating workers are self motivated. They like to supervise themselves.
4. With employees' participation, the work environment and organizational culture improves.

6.13.4 Rewards and Recognition: The process of human resource development begins with recruitment of right the person into the organization for the specific job and proceeds with training. The management leadership should aim at integrating individuals to the system and motivating for better performance. Some experts suggest that appraisal plays key role in developing, improving individual performance. Deming along with many others consider individual performance appraisal is not consistent with total quality. They argue that the variation should appropriately be attributed to system rather than individuals [22] and emphasize on training and development essential for the implementation of total quality.

The basic element of hiring in any business organization is remuneration package-to provide wage/salary for employee's maintenance and security in lieu of his commitment to the work and organization. The incentive system is generally designed for better performance. These include profit share-linking payment for achievement of profit target, individual merit pay by way of merit increment, individual and team bonus-a part of the company's profit.

HRM bases its decision on the output of a worker on the shop floor in a manufacturing organization and on the 'customer service index' in a setup providing service: assessing employee's response in answering the phone, handling customer complaints, punctuality, quality of overall service and others specific to requirement. These incentive schemes underpin development of service quality. Critics however find that they offer little in the strategic integration and prove by and large ineffective to 'buy' commitment to quality.

Quality experts also confirm that financial incentives marginally contribute towards the implementation of TQM and they can in fact be counterproductive. Crosby (1979) suggests, that to reward an employee's commitment to quality with financial incentives is to risk demeaning them, by attaching a price tag to his sincerity. He claims that recognition is the key and recommends quality awards and prizes. Peer nomination for such award is a novel practice for encouraging motivation. [23]

Deming (1986) goes even further, considers use of performance appraisal and management by objectives as one of the 'deadly diseases' of western management. He characterizes this approach as 'management by fear' and concludes that what organization may at best expect is limited to short-term performance like meeting targets. This style of functioning militates against the idea of co-operation and team work espoused in quality management. It undermines creative and committed behaviour necessary for a quality organization.

Japan is first to introduce a scheme for national award for quality excellence. The objectives: first, to create a competitive spirit amongst the producers, and second, to honour Deming for his contribution to development designating the award as 'Deming Prize'. The system was adopted in USA as the Malcolm Baldrige National Quality Award and in Europe as the European Foundation for Quality Management Award each with its own variations.

6.14 Implementation Strategy

Quality literature also suggests that implementation strategy in respect of each company must be unique, specifically modelled to suit its present status and the requirement. An optimal approach based on the best-in-practice models that have been successful in industry is synthesized for providing guidance. It is a schedule—what should come first and what follows next. It is recommended to be flexible for adaptation. The dynamic business environment demands flexibility and the managers implementing the project should ensure that it best fits the process with suitable adjustment. It happens in practice that different departments of the same organization require separate strategy for accomplishing the organizational goal.

Broadly the implementation is divided into three phases: the preparation phase, the planning phase and execution phase and the steps involved in each phase are discussed below.

6.14.1 Preparation Phase: Preparation follows with commitment of time, resource and involvement in the following time sequenced steps.

Step 1: Total Quality Steering Committee-Formation: The top executive selects the members to form the Quality Steering Committee (QSC) with himself as the leader. QSC should act as a management board for introduction, development and direction of quality programme in the organization.

Step 2: Total Quality Steering Committee-Team

Building: The members are trained on team building session conducted by an expert, preferably an outsider. The committee members must be aware of their role as a team assigned with decision making for implementing projects. It is an essential prerequisite.

Step 3: Training of Members: The members also require training on total quality philosophy, concepts and systems for proper application. Training by qualified and experienced expert/consultant is preferable.

Step 4: Developing a Vision Statement on Total Quality: The management discusses and finalizes a vision statement that embodies the hopes and aspirations of all involved with the company. It is an important document to be the guiding principle throughout the implementation.

Step 5: Establishment of Broad Objectives: The QSC translates the vision into a set of broad strategic objectives with schedules and targets after detailed deliberation and consensus.

Step 6: Communication and Publicity: The employees should be fully informed about the project being implemented rather than speculating it. The communication must contain detailed information about the company's vision, broad objectives, strategies and the expected outcome of the total quality implementation. Open communication helps to enlist commitment of almost all employees, with their active participation for further improvement. It reinforces open management style.

Step 7: Strength and Weakness of the Organization (SWOT) Analysis: A strength and weakness, opportunity and threat analysis of the company is undertaken objectively to evaluate the deficiencies and weak areas to act upon and prospects to rely on.

Step 8: Identifying Advocates and Resistors: Identification of the key people who support the programme and those who are likely to oppose it is necessary. The QSC members may keep this information in view while selecting the project implementation team and subsequently to ascertain the reasons of the concerns of the resistors and communicate with them to dispel their doubts (QFD technique is relevant).

Step 9: Assessment of Employee Attitudes: The attitudes of employees are of paramount importance to the organization. An assessment with advanced techniques would provide the present state and similar assessment after implementation will show the effectiveness of establishing total quality culture in the organization.

Step 10: Feedback on Customer satisfaction: Similarly, the present level of customer satisfaction before and after implementation will evidence the result. The marketing and marketing research department may undertake the exercise for monitoring total quality efforts in objective realization (i.e., customer satisfaction).

6.14.2 Planning Phase:

Step 11: Planning Approach (PDCA Cycle): Planning for implementation of total quality is a very important step because it becomes continuous after the initial PCDA cycle for course correction based on feedback, taking up new projects with the experience. Once total quality is in motion, the step effectively shifts to operate within the PDCA cycle, as originated by Shewhart (Walton, 1986:87).

Step 12: Project Selection: The steering committee takes into account the vision, broad objectives of the company including its strength and weakness and selects the project that is of utmost priority that would result in positive results-increased profitability, customer satisfaction (refer step 10). The first experience should be inspiring for motivating all. At this point, there should be a communication blitz.

Step 13: Team Composition: Consequent to selection of the project, it is the responsibility of the QSC to select the task team. Care need to be taken that the team is represented by competent personnel from all related departments, such as production, design, marketing, quality.

Step 14: Team Training: The selected members of the

team have to undergo intensive training by an expert. They require not the basic but in-depth knowledge on the implication of total quality implementation and the outcome.

6.14.3 Execution Phase:

Step 15: Action on the Project: The team works on the project as per the guidance of the steering committee. Their knowledge on tools, techniques help achieving successful implementation.

Step 16: Team Feedback: During the process of implementation of the project, the team provides feedback to the steering committee on a regular basis. And the QSC, based on the feedback, advises action to be taken.

Step 17: Customer Feedback: As the project gets implemented, it is necessary to collect customer reaction. The marketing department collects the information which is analyzed and evaluated to monitor progress.

Step 18: Employee Feedback: The change in the attitude of employees is also important. It is useful for the management to ascertain the effectiveness of total quality in the organization.

Step 19: Evaluation and Action: Based on the report on the evaluation of customer satisfaction, employees attitude, rate of waste generation (defects, re-work) the steering committee takes decision in regard to standardizing the process, procedure or changing them.

6.15 Some Concerns

A large volume of publication on quality is available today. These relate to the concepts, systems, tools, techniques and management approaches for achieving total quality in a business enterprise. These are being enriched continuously by research and innovative application in industry. The results of total quality implementation, as researches reveal, offer an interesting pattern: a wide spectrum is generally satisfied, some are too happy where as a few are sceptical due to poor results or dismal failure.

Analysis of the instances where the results have not been

what TQM espoused evince with sufficient proof that failures are not in the concept or tools, but in the method of implementation and that some of the common differentiators between success and failure are commitment, knowledge and expertise to guide implementation for improvement. The fluid state spells lack of management in particular; the processes and systems that need to be properly managed for quality have not been taken care of adequately. The major reasons are attributable to the following:

1. The major problem in many companies is decrease in sales. When analyzed, it is found in most cases that there has been improper specification-the specification does not satisfy the most critical parameters that meet the customer requirements. This is due to the reluctance of the senior management to understand fully the system of design and development process that provide characteristics like reliability, maintainability, safety.
2. The management, senior as well as the middle level are driven by short-term consideration such as achieving production targets at any cost rather than long-term gains. The attitude to focus on immediate problem and anxious to secure 'quick-fix' solutions fails to improve the processes to the desired level.
3. The management does not appreciate that the quality of output is directly or indirectly dependent upon many participating constituents, i.e. departments and functions. And in practice, some of these are effectively controlled while others are not.
4. Inertia of the management to change their traditional style of functioning,
5. The workers dislike to implement change because of the procedural complexity [24] and lack of interest on the part of management to provide required education and training for empowerment.
6. Sometimes, selection of consultants who are not adequately equipped with management acumen,

application of tools and techniques also aggravate the problem.

The scope of change/improvement desired too has paramount effect on outcome; for example, some suggest Big Bang type transformation where as other advocate strategy for incremental change. It is because, they believe, gradual improvement in the quality cultures is more effective. It is however seen in practice that each approach has its advantage and judicious application to suit the situation is crucial for success. [25] Experiences in the past have been interesting: the quality circles do not work well in every enterprise (and are even discouraged by some managers), and relatively few ISO certified enterprises have won the national quality awards.

For example, the American industry introduced quality circle in mid-1980s but could not achieve desired result, because it was not properly planned, structured for focus-lack of clear objective. Management was eager to keep score by number of teams deployed, because it was difficult to develop meaningful numbers in terms of increased profitability, customer satisfaction, reduction of waste-all attributable to total quality. No one knew what they were doing, except spending money (Geotsch and Davis, 1994:583). This was in contrast to what Ohno achieved at Toyota plant, Japan by introducing quality circle concept.

The operators, supervisors possessing knowledge, skill and experience of the process formed a small team to discuss how to solve problems, improve the product features, manufacturing process and reduce defects. It was result oriented, focused on continuous improvement. And this became the genesis of an important technique, *Kaizen* in quality management. [26] It offers clear example how programme should be successfully implemented for organizational gains, which the industry can emulate.

6.16 Cautions in Implementation

The criticality of the implementation process as discussed suggests that success lies in the pragmatic application management approaches keeping in view not only the product but also the people and the socio-cultural environment. In fact, the systems and sub-systems involve simply too many variables and lack of full awareness and implications by those who take decisions results in inappropriate implementation for total quality. The implementing team therefore needs to consider carefully which approach is best suited for the concerned unit.

Learning from the experience, it is worth adopting such practices which have proved to be effective. Some important aspects which need to be considered are as follows:

1. **Don't rush to total quality, implement only when the company is ready:** The first step to implement total quality programme in any organisation is to educate the managers, supervisors and workers on the subject of total quality in order that they are in a position to understand the prerequisite for successful implementation, i.e. top management commitment, sincere involvement of employees and above all the fact that benefits accrue in the long run, that is the outcomes may not be visible immediately.
2. **Don't delegate in the project implementation:** Experiences also evidence that full participation of top executive and managers are essential for successful implementation of total quality. Delegation, by and large, has resulted in failures. Thus, the management should not only commit to provide resources but also devote time. Juran suggests that senior management must be involved in performing certain types of strategic activities themselves as opposed to delegating them to subordinates.
3. **Don't train all employees at once:** Training is an essential element of the process but it has to be planned properly, structured by experts and scheduled as per requirement. Employees generally find it discouraging if they learn devoting time and energy and no scope for using it. They also tend to forget if not applied to practice.

It becomes a negative motivating factor.

4. **Avoid uncertainty syndrome:** A usual problem that an organization faces during transition process is the inability of the management to envisage outcome and prepare sufficiently ahead to deal with it. The uncertainty could be avoided with complete information on all aspects collected in a systematic manner, preferably by professionals and sharing with all involved. It helps everyone in the company, management to employees, well prepared to accept a new philosophy and transit.

Drucker's advice is relevant in this context; 'To start this turn around thus requires a willingness to rethink and to re-examine the company's business policy and practice. It requires stopping saying "we know" and instead saying "let's ask". And there are two sets of questions that need to be asked. First, who are the customers and who are the non-customers? What is value to them? What do they pay for? Second, what do they [successful companies] do that we do not do? What do they not do that we know is essential? What do they assume that we know to be wrong?'

The basic components of the system need to be re-modelled, to begin with appropriate organization structure-designed to be effective. The focus shifts from formal bureaucratic task based pyramid design for flow of instructions and delegation to process oriented flatten structure that uses team to manage everything: maximizing supplier and customer contact, customer satisfaction driving output. The model is based on interdependence to foster motivation, easier flow of communication essential for an improved working environment. Better team efforts are rewarding.

There is also need for creating an enabling work environment in response to the changing needs. Changes are situational—a job transfer, a new place, a new assignment and the like, where as transition is a psychological process that people go through when they must come in terms with a new situation.

The senior management must put quality goals into the strategic objectives, implement quality policy with suitable action plan, adopt 'Big Q' concept, provide leadership, organize training at all levels and mandate use of structured quality planning in lieu of empiricism. [27]

End Notes

1. Juran in *'Juran on Leadership for Quality'* notes, 'all large organizations exhibit some of the features of a biological organism. Invariably one of these features is the immune reaction when something alien is introduced. The organism senses the intrusion of the alien and mobilises to reject it' (p.192).
2. A more inclusive definition of leadership by Alan Keith of Genentech states that, 'Leadership is ultimately about creating a way for people to contribute to making something extraordinary happen.'
3. George, Stephen and Arnold Weimerskirch '*Total Quality Management*' John Wiley and Sons, 1994.
4. Stephen Covey's '*Seven Habits of Highly Effective People*' provides an insight to developing leadership style by using inside-out perspective, moving from the individual level to interpersonal relations and then to managerial responsibilities and organizational values. Townsend and Gebhardt in *'Quality in Action'* conclude that 'leadership for quality must be active, obvious and informed' (p.9).
5. Townsend and Gebhardt in *'Quality in Action'* conclude that 'leadership for quality must be active, obvious and informed' (p. 9).
6. Watson, Thomas J. Jr. '*A Business and its Beliefs-The ideas that helped build IBM*' McGraw Hill, New York, 2003.
7. Sagan, Carl '*Broca's Brain*' Random House, 1979: ch. 2.
8. Townsend and Gebhardt in '*Quality in Action*' conclude that, 'partial understanding of and involvement in quality can produce only partial success or total failure. Complete success requires complete process. The only chance for a quality process to truly succeed is for a company to simultaneously attack all the issues: leadership, participation and measurement' (p. 17).
9. Refer Anderson (1994) on 'the world class company', Lawler (1986) on 'the high commitment organization', Peters and

*Waterman (1982) on 'best practice organization' for detailed discussion on the issue.

10. A problem is simply the performance which varies from what is expected in an undesirable way.
11. Juran in '*Juran on Leadership for Quality*' asserts that 'chief among the realities is the fact that the upper managers must participate personally and extensively in the effort'.
12. Refer '*Juran on Leadership for Quality*' for a detailed discussion on 'Big Q' and 'Little Q', Understanding the difference helps in selection of a project.
13. Merli in '*Total Quality Management*' lists twenty strategies for continuous improvement which he describes as 'The Twenty Organising Points of Total manufacturing management' (1009: 163).
14. A tangible product is any physical product that can be seen, touched like a computer, automobile and an intangible product is a non-physical product like an insurance policy. In retailing, products are called merchandise. Commodities are usually raw materials such as metals and agricultural produce, but a commodity can also be anything widely available in the open market.
15. Wyatt, John, 'T*he New Deal: What Companies and Employees owe each other*' Fortune, June 13, 1994.
16. Sri Aurobindo writes, 'self-attainment is the secret and self-knowledge is the means in the development process'.
17. Oakland, J.S., '*Total Quality Management: The Route to Improving Performance*' Butterworth-Heinemann, 1993.
18. John Ruskin, Pre-Raphaelitism (1851).
19. Extending specification beyond product and into the realm of operator performance was the first attempt to define the 'extended system of operations' which would greatly facilitate the production process (Lindsay and Petrick, 1997: 66).
20. Sandholm in '*Japanese Quality Circle*' concludes that 'if one or more of the conditions have not been met, the operator cannot be blamed: this is a management controllable defect' (p. 22).
21. A KPMG Peat Marwick Survey, 1991 also found that 'while training was the most important initiative in the early stages of total quality implementation, cross functional quality teams and work process redesign became relatively more important in more mature implementations'.

22. Fletcher in '*Appraisal: Routes to Improved Performance*' too reject traditional assessment based approach.
23. Reward goes beyond benefits and salaries to the belief 'we are family' and 'we do excellent work' (Scholtes, 1992: 12).
24. Reger et al. (1994) throw a different perspective on why total quality efforts often fail: 'the theory suggests that employees resist total quality because their belief about the organization's identity constrain understanding and create cognitive opposition to radical change'.
25. In this context, Reger et al. (1994) suggest that, 'Implementation may best be accomplished through a series of middle-range changes that are large enough to overcome cognitive inertia and relieve an organization stress, but not so large that members believe the proposed change is unattainable or undesirable.'
26. There have been well publicized failures of BPR, as well as Six Sigma including their successes.
27. Juran, J.M., 'Juran on Quality by Design: The New Steps for Planning Quality into Goods and Services' Free Press, New York, 1992: 496.

7

Stages of Quality Journey

We have discussed at some length that introduction of total quality system in a business enterprise should be with a clear objective: to offer products and services that meet and exceed customer expectations. And as a result, it benefits the organization as a whole. Research findings overwhelmingly support the hypothesis and experiences too evince that companies implementing total quality programmes have gained phenomenal success. It has proved to be the most preferred means for improving competitiveness in product, enhancing brand image and increasing goodwill. The benefits are not only limited to intangible assets creation, but also raises profitability by better performance because quality, productivity and efficiency are interconnected. [1]

Implementation of the total quality system however entails pragmatic application of quality tools, techniques and approach for attaining success. And on implementation, it would ensure that:

1. The processes are under control, i.e. the output as per desired quality and wastages eliminated or substantially reduced.
2. The employees are empowered through education and training for their full involvement and participation.
3. It promises to encourage 'internal partnering' [2], a culture that would motivate every individual in the organization to recognize that customer satisfaction and business objectives are inseparable and work sincerely towards improvement for the greater good of the organization, and
4. Conducive work environment are created to foster teamwork and contribute towards improvement of productivity and efficiency.

The companies in the industrialized countries like the United States, European Union and Japan are increasingly adopting total quality practices, investing on further research and developing newer approaches.

The experience should be a good starting point for Indian companies to introduce quality management system for achieving excellence in product and service quality.

7.1 The Indian Context

Pre-Independence (specifically during the British rule) India suffered heavily. Even the indigenous industry could not sustain, despite many comparative advantages. Post-Independence, industry in India has progressed and the growth has been substantial. The development to date encompasses wide range of products including high tech products catering to the domestic requirement as well as exports. The present status, however, weighs heavily on foreign technology support and entrepreneurship. A wide section believes that the growth has not been to India's potential. And in particular, the development of quality culture has not been to the desired extent. The reasons vary:

1. The public sector which has been nurtured with state policy and financial support for the development of items primary to the economy developed a sense of complacency. Though they too have started facing competition, the management attitude for adopting modern corporate culture is still lacking, perhaps due to government support.
2. The bulk of the industrial units being in the small scale sector are subject to inherent problems of resource limitation (capital, technology) in addition to professional management and continue with ad hoc style of functioning.
3. Yet another section, which have the benefit of foreign capital and technology, tend to be content with and remain fully dependent on collaborator's assistance rather than

investing to independently carry forward further development as Japan did.

Despite India's potent advantage, investment in research and development has been very low in comparison to other developed countries. As a result, a comparison of the quality of most of our products with that of industrialized countries is rather difficult. However, viewing from a broader perspective, it would be safe to conclude that Indian manufacturing sector has so far progressed from inspection to standardization phase in quality journey. Thus, implementation of quality management system is logically the next step.

The quality initiatives, in a true professional sense, started in India in 1980s ostensibly reflecting a growing recognition of the importance of effective management of critical factors as a source of competitive advantage consequent on economic liberalization that introduced international competition. It did spread but remained confined to a few units due to various reasons. And in the context of managing for quality in Indian industry, a discussion follows.

The people of India have an earnest desire to fulfil the 'Indian Dream' that India develops to be a great economic power and enjoys its rightful place in the gallery of nations. The development experience presents a clear picture: policy liberalization is necessary but not sufficient. The state need to provide an open policy regime and the enterprises must adopt and adapt modern techniques in order to exploit comparative advantages to its favour. One of the proven paths for achieving success seems, as it has been discussed earlier, is introduction of quality systems at unit level. It is imperative to regain, sustain and enhance market position including venturing a global presence, for quality is essentially an in-company activity.

A company therefore should begin the quality journey in the right direction following a sound quality philosophy: introducing quality policy and objective; quality improvement programme with proper systems for quality planning, design and development, supplier survey, process capability analysis, inspection planning, quality audit, quality data feedback, quality cost analysis and so on. And notwithstanding the diversity of the structure of our industry and its inherent complexity, there seems tremendous scope and potential for the companies including those in the small and medium sector to implement quality measures in order to get the benefits of developing quality culture in the organization and become world class producers of goods and services. Some industry associations have started focussing on quality as a system for improvement and it must spread.

The improvement programme being influenced by various internal and external factors, one model for all is rather difficult. Thus, a synthesis of theoretical concepts, tools and techniques and practical experience is presented as a guideline for the practicing managers interested in introducing or thinking of introducing quality system in industry.

7.2 Essential Prerequisite

The journey must begin with top management's conviction and resolve: conviction that quality improvement programme is essentially required for achieving the organizational goal and their resolve for excellence; for example, 'we shall be the best company in the country/region in the area of our activity' and commit to provide resource for the same.

It sets the vision for the enterprise and inspires confidence in the organization. Then the lead team [3] redefines the company's philosophy in keeping with the vision and quantifies goals to be accomplished in a definite time frame. Having set the objectives, it is necessary to choose the right approach. And the right approach is careful preparation for a successful quality journey.

The first step of the journey is preparation of a report by the 'task team' on the company's present status, potential for market expansion identifying areas that require improvement and more importantly an analysis of the projected financial data with and without implementing projects for improvement. A comprehensive future outcome may convince the senior management, for they only appreciate the language of money.

The problem of quality has always been top management's lack of understanding of their responsibility for causing a cultural change in the organization as a whole to bring about improvement in product quality and prevention of controllable defects in the processes. [4] The management's understanding is essential. Some basic knowledge about the product, process and customers in addition to a broad overview of the company's systems and functioning especially the key areas that contribute to quality. It empowers them to appreciate and objectively decide:

1. The actions necessary to achieve continual improvement,
2. The sequence and interaction of the processes,
3. The tools and techniques need to be deployed to bring the processes and systems under control for quality output,
4. The requirement of resources to support the implementation of projects for improvement,
5. The need for an effective measuring system for monitoring the progress, and
6. Establishing a system of communication for the management and employees.

The management then decides to organize teams with qualified personnel dedicated to specific assignment for the implementation of the project. [5]

7.3 Developing a Vision and Mission

The management should deftly decide and take necessary action for establishing a long-term vision for the organization. It must be based on facts and consensus. A vision statement defines where the organization intends to go—a clear picture of the desired future position. [6] A well conceived mission statement provides the institutional purpose for the legitimate existence of the organization and describes distinctively what sets it apart from others in its area of activity. It encompasses a broader perspective to facilitate quality growth and also at the same time to focus the organization on what it does best. And once the vision of the future is shared and endorsed, the scanning of the current situation permits a comparison between what exists and what should exist for achieving desired result. In order to fulfil its vision, the organization builds these into a clear business strategy thereby deriving the project objectives in a specific time frame.

In a total quality organization, service to stakeholders, dedication to continuous improvement, application of scientific tools and techniques, measurement and control for system improvement, empowerment and respect for people and personal integrity are core values. These aspects being key determinants for performance improvement should form the basis of the mission for the organization and its employees. And the values are created by design and endorsed by participation and consensus, rather than default.

7.4 Defining Quality Objective

A business unit defines its quality objective, sets quantified targets in the long-, medium- and short-term [7] in order to achieve improvement in quality of its output and there by delighting customers. The quality objectives that aim at continuous improvement by eliminating chronic level of quality deficiencies may include the following:

1. The cross functional quality objective—product and service design should take into account the feedback from customers received by marketing department and the quality department must analyze process capability for making quality product.
2. The cost objective—right price of product/service for the customer and profit for the organization.
3. The delivery objective—to ensure that right product/services are delivered at right time in right quantity, as per schedule.
4. The safety objective—adequate provisioning for safety of

product when in use.

5. The service objective—to monitor providing stated after sales service.
6. The innovation objective—to work individually and along with the team for breakthrough in technology for product/process development.
7. The measurement objective—systematic quantification and comparison of an organization's product/service with that of market leaders. This helps to get information where the organization stands and action to be taken for improvement for enhancing competitive position.
8. The ethical objective—for an unblemished reputation that the organization does not compromise on principle.

Clearly written objectives are essential prerequisite for planned improvement. The document is communicated to all for information and action. It becomes binding with the stamp of authority, helps to unify the thinking of managers in different departments and stimulates action.

7.5 Quality Policy

The management in order to achieve set objective develops appropriate a quality policy which:

1. Includes a commitment to comply with requirements and continually improve the effectiveness of the quality management system.
2. Provides a framework for establishing and reviewing quality objectives.
3. Should be communicated to and understood by all within the company.
4. must be reviewed keeping in view the information collected from customers, quality control data so that the policy statement is appropriate to the changing needs.

The statement, for example, could be: *'(Company Name) is committed to meeting and exceeding customer needs and preferences. Supplying quality product, on-time and at a competitive price is company's responsibility. It will be achieved through the total quality system in accordance with the requirements of the ISO 9001:2008.'*

A written policy document developed by consensus forms the basis for all concerned to take action and the management to monitor performance. It forces the managers to think out in depth and develop solutions to their problems. It also facilitates the audit of practice against policy-measurement for monitoring performance.

7.6 Formulating Strategy

A total quality strategy is the intended and realised pattern of organizational guidance and the development of structure and management processes that produce total customer satisfaction (Lindsay and Petrick, 1997:91). And developing a comprehensive model requires synthesis of hard data and soft insight. Having set the objective to establish a total quality organization, the process would entail grafting new systems into the existing one. It involves a total transformation of the organization and it is well known that managing change is always a challenge. Thus, programme implementation to be successful; it has to be structured, well organized and systematic. Strategic planning and management are crucial. And the onus rests on the management to deftly handle with suitable approach. [8] And a customer value driven approach seems more appropriate to deal with quality improvement and it comprises the following four basic elements:

1. **Strategic Planning:** The process involves assessment of the firm's strength and weakness that exists within and external environment analysis of opportunity and threat in order to survive and adapt to the current reality.
2. **Strategy formulation:** It requires full information on the internal and external environmental factors and well as intuitive judgment which the management can get from the operational experience of the exceptional managers. [9] A synthesis of hard data and the soft insight helps developing a more pragmatic approach.

3. **Strategy Implementation:** Is very important in the sense that the success depends the way a plan is translated into action.
4. **Evaluation and control:** A system to measure and determine the efficacy of the implementation. It provides information on the complete chain encompassing inputs, processes to output and customer feedback.

Regular review ensures that quality strategy continues to be focused on priority objectives, limits non-value added functions and fine-tunes the work processes for better results. The managers must collect unbiased data and utilize it for continuous improvement. The attention of the leadership is drawn for decision as and when required.

The strategy for implementing new initiative therefore should be systemic adopting fundamental principles, concepts, tools and techniques for managing change. The lead team assigned with the task of project implementation should be properly trained by experts. A pragmatic decision based on objective assessment is needed to decide whether available skill within is adequate or to employ an external consultant.

It is necessary to take specialized services offered by consultants and. experts when introducing a new system, particularly where the relevant skills and expertise are not available within the organization. They offer unbiased and independent advice for deciding correct approach and optimally allocating valuable resources. The use of consultants, even on a temporary basis, becomes a viable solution when new initiatives and improvements are intended to boost the existing quality system, or improve upon the systems and processes.

The external consultant may prove useful, for it is supposed to take an unbiased view of the status and requirement for achieving quality objective. A careful selection of the agency is essential. It is like choosing a *guru* for a disciple in olden days, for the quality of training entirely depends on the calibre of the teacher. A proper selection requires sound judgment of the top management to identify the best amongst the available and that they are willing to take up assignment with commitment for long-term engagement.

7.7 Consultant Selection

There are various types of experts and consultants available in the market; most have the skills needed to facilitate improvement activities such as quality control, auditing and procedural documentation. More experienced consultants are likely to have knowledge of specialized methods for quality improvement that cover product improvement, process improvement and people based improvement for introduction of quality programme with application of quality tools and techniques. Consultants having previous experience, having undertaken similar project may offer advantage.

While on one side they can be an effective agent of change, on the other side they may find it difficult to get details of the internal working, background, processes involved including cultural factors that are critical to initiate required change. A few even may apply a 'canned solution', collect the fee and fly out leaving the actual implementation to follow. It is to be noted that implementation of a total quality management system in an organization generally takes long time, as it must be facilitated at every level of the organization and each and every stage of implementation. Thus, the expert service should be available on a long-term engagement with client for in-depth analysis, timely assistance for appropriate decision-making, monitoring and following up progress.

7.7.1 Engaging with Consultant: Client-consultant engagement should be comprehensive. This is essential for deriving benefit from total quality. The company implementing improvement project expects the consultant to offer expert advice on: (a) the identification of business need based on internal assessment, deploying benchmarking technique, (b) prioritising project as per Pareto principle, (c) planning and preparation for action, (d) developing strategy, (e) implementation of the project, (f) periodic review based on measurement for evaluation, and (g) effecting course correction, if required. The key contributions expected from the consultant are:

1. Facilitating knowledge transfer to the client on the systems, processes, tools and techniques required for improvement through specialized training.
2. Developing empowered team for implementation for high performance.
3. Establishing sound systems and procedure for performance evaluation with appropriate measurement standards.
4. Introducing a reporting system for management and employees at all levels about the progress as a matter of practice.
5. Assessing the impact of the project and follow up action needed for continuous improvement.

In addition, the consultant should also develop a suitable data base with information technology tools to facilitate knowledge storage and retrieval. It helps in repeatability of usage and improves accuracy in measurement and evaluation.

7.8 In-house Expertise

A corporation generally has access to knowledge and skills in-house and in case, the management feels confident that the available expertise can take up the task of implementing total quality programme, a lead team of key personnel must be formed and assigned with the responsibility along with adequate authority. The members, if considered necessary may also be trained for updating their skill set. They may refresh the existing level of knowledge from the huge volume of literature available on quality management. For example, Peters and Waterman (1992) advocate eight common themes which they argue are responsible for success: [10]

1. A bias for action: active decision-making—'getting on with it'.

2. Close to the customer: learning from the people served by the business.
3. Autonomy and entrepreneurship: fostering innovation and nurturing 'champions'.
4. Productivity through people: treating rank and file employees as a source of quality.
5. Hands-on, value-driven management philosophy: to guide everyday practice and management showing its commitment.
6. Stick to the knitting: stay with the business that you know.
7. Simple form, lean staff: some of the best companies have minimal HQ staff.
8. Simultaneous loose-tight properties: autonomy in shop-floor activities plus centralised values.

These however primarily focus on concepts, systems and procedures which tend to overwhelm not only the students but the practitioners alike, sometimes creating varied perceptions particularly regarding implementation for success.

7.9 Getting Started

An outline for preparation, prior to implementation, that is, how a business unit must prepare for implementing total quality programme is provided above. The quality concepts, tools and systems are discussed in the previous chapters. These aspects are blended with results from the long years practical experiences to form a practical approach that a manufacturing unit should be concerned with to proceed for establishing total quality system in the organization.

The approach however should be developed for specific goal and would depend on many influencing factors like the company's activity status, the level of quality, overall environment including employee's motivation among others. The lead team must design a programme in consultation with key personnel specific to meet the need.

They must rely on information generally available from: (a) the quality level of the product is expressed in the final inspection and quality audit as percent defective and in number of demerits respectively, and (b) the performance record and reports on external failure comprising customer complaints, after sales/service, warranty, call back and user re-action. Analysis of complaint rate and cost per unit of product under guarantee also provide useful data. In addition, feedback received from customers, either written or verbal are vital inputs. The useful information are analysed and the data must guide strategic planning.

In case of a manufacturing unit, there could be distinctly two scenarios: (i) improving the quality of an existing product or (ii) launching of a new product, including modification of an existing product by way of product diversification. While decision to introducing a new product in the market would depend heavily on the demand carefully studied by the market research department and the design department incorporating the customers' needs at the preliminary design stage itself (ref. QFD), improvement of existing activity entails remedial action for eliminating causes of a problem to bring about changes so that the processes and systems are under control for quality output along with wastage reduction (ref. Juran's Trilogy). The objectives and boundary conditions in two cases being different, the approach to improvement has to be specifically designed. These are discussed in detail.

7.10 Quality Improvement

The quality improvement sequence in the existing business organization is a course of action that begins with the selection of a project, analysis of symptom and passes through identification of cause to remedial action. It aims at elimination (or, at least substantial reduction) of defects in the manufacturing processes and systems. The control chart would reveal defects which could either be sporadic or chronic in nature. While sporadic defects in the manufacture are easy to remedy, chronic defects requires greater effort to find root cause for eliminating them.

The first step of the process is to collect information on quality of output available from the final inspection, product quality audit and data relating to failures, complaints, returns, after sales service. The control charts provide sufficient evidences about the nature of problems, which could be remedied with application of appropriate measures. In addition, discussion with key personnel at the work station— operator, supervisor, in related departments is very useful. The evaluation guides action.

7.10.1 Sporadic Problem: The course of action to deal with sporadic and minor defects is much simpler. When such defects occur, these are normally noticed instantly from the control chart at the work station (ref. control chart in chapter 4) and the operators at the factory floor along with supervisor can easily find a solution. It is part of their job to set the manufacturing process in order as a matter of routine. In fact, finding a remedy is within their area of responsibility. It does not require any extra effort as it is considered to be their normal work. In exceptional cases, assistance of the specialists and the quality department may be called for.

7.10.2 Chronic Problems: The problems that have assumed chronic proportion are likely to involve several departments within the company or even external factors like quality of procured inputs. The root cause may be attributable to a number of inter-related processes and systems or sub systems. The problems being complex, planning for improvement of this kind necessitates better understanding, knowledge of the total system, functions of various departments and their inter relation. That a problem has assumed chronic state does not necessarily mean that the company lacks knowledge and expertise to timely rectify the process defect which has resulted in huge wastages (that is the burden of cost to the company); it may rather be due to lack of a clearly expressed responsibility as to who should do what or lack of top management initiative to take up improvement measures.

This means that in addition to quality approach (quality tools, techniques and their application), managing coordination of various departments contributing to quality is essential. Some experts suggest, for example, Juran's Trilogy, that reduction of chronic defects is better achieved by a breakthrough, where as others like Ishikawa's *Kaizen* advocates incremental improvement as more suitable. All these approaches have been found equally effective in quality improvement, calling for pragmatic application depending on the functional status of the company- its activities, problem areas that need immediate attention along with employees' motivation. An organization for improvement takes care of these shortcomings in order to achieve a breakthrough. The programme would depend to a large extent on the company's activities, its size, management philosophy including traditions and culture. In any event, the improvement process would result in:

1. Achieving control of the processes in manufacture for quality output.
2. Eventual elimination or substantial reduction of wastages.

The managing team should then follow-up and monitor to hold the gains. Important steps are explained below.

To begin with, it is necessary to find the strength and weakness, opportunity and threats of the company and especially why the profitability of the company is affected. The factors that must be looked into in great details during the evaluation of the quality activities in the company include the following:

1. The quality of the company's product in comparison with that of its competitors.
2. Benchmarking with respect to weak areas that need improvement.
3. Motivation of the company to offer product of high quality along with its safety and reliability.
4. Measures that would result in reduction of cost.

The team assigned with the improvement programme

implementation should get a clear picture of all the processes and systems in the organization for formulating action plan to attain desired improvement. The senior management should appreciate that the control of the overall activity in the company is the responsibility of all departments contributing to quality and the employees at all levels. The message should be clearly communicated to all that success of a quality improvement programme would depend on proper coordination amongst all the functions directly or indirectly contributing to enhancement of productivity.

7.11 Quality Committee for Co-ordination

The progress of quality system implementation also requires periodic review. As top management is generally occupied with various responsibilities, a forum may be created with specific assignment to oversee and evaluate performance of the improvement project. It could be a 'quality committee' or the work can also be assigned to the existing 'management committee' in the organization. The committee's responsibility is not to solve the problem, but to see to it that the project under implementation for solving the problems are moving in the right direction and on schedule. The members of the committee should be responsible persons from the related functional departments and given authority to take decisions when required. Their work would include the following:

1. Evaluation of the quality problems that need to be solved.
2. Select project for improvement assigning priority.
3. Allocate required resources for project implementation.
4. Form 'task team' for taking actions.
5. Take decisions on the measures suggested by the team.
6. Monitoring of progress for follow up with review reports on the project implementation.
7. Reporting the gains to the top management (board of directors of the company) and inform all employees in the organization.

They should be capable of carrying through the measures

and continue monitoring with measurement and control. The task team and quality committee being represented by all concerned departments, it offers many advantages:

1. The team members can easily widen their knowledge by discussions, better appreciate the implication of the improvement process and outcome there of.
2. It is always seen that some accept change, for they understand logically the technical aspects where as others are willing to accept the measure as right by group consensus. It is an avenue for all departments to work in coeval with organizational goal.
3. In case there are other persons responsible for implementing change, they could be inducted to the group as members for facilitating faster implementation.
4. It is easier for the members to motivate the employees in their respective department for smooth implementation. Resistance, if any can be handled by the management.
5. All departments work for accomplishing the common goal and thus leave no scope for sub-optimization in the organization.
6. The involvement of all sections would promote a culture, that is quality culture.

7.12 Improvement Process

Improving the overall performance of an enterprise with dramatic changes in its systems and functions demands an entirely new approach since the traditional practice has not resulted in the desired result. The team assigned to take responsibility for successful implementation should be equipped with knowledge and expertise for diagnosis of the problem, identification of the root cause and finding a solution set that would eliminate the cause for improved performance. In order to bring about such change, there is need for re-orientation of management attitude, application of technology, gaining knowledge in advanced tools and techniques, adoption of modern style of functioning and investment in training for empowerment.

In general, improvement process follows a special sequence—the universal sequence of steps for improving product quality, reducing chronic defects and wastages and these are:

7.12.1 Data Collection: Normally, volumes of information are available within the organization; the control chart at the work station or quality department, regular data on defects, rework, call back with the quality/marketing department and feedback from the customers with marketing. The information should be properly collated and categorized in terms of their seriousness and in relation to the product and process. The fact sheet must form the basis for prioritising the project to be taken up for improvement.

7.12.2 Selection of Project: Based on the data, the quality problems are assigned priority—defects most costly or most frequent must attract immediate attention. The cost burden due to defects in production or costs of failures over a period of time are analysed on Pareto principle (considering vital few as against the trivial many) for selection of the project for improvement.

The list of possible areas set for remedial action can sometimes be long. The quality committee is presented with a list of projects that are most beneficial to the organization along with the following details in respect of each:

1. Measures required to be taken.
2. Resources required including external technical support, if any.
3. Expected result.
4. Time frame for completion.

The report should also include the estimates of costs involved and gains expected. A financial balance sheet is better appreciated by the top management. The best way to achieve success in improving quality is application of Juran's Trilogy: improvement has to proceed project by project and project selected strictly in accordance with Pareto Principle.

7.12.3 Identification of Root Cause: In certain cases, the causes are obvious where as some defects may be complex. The root cause may relate to more than one system or subsystem. There is possibility that many trials have not resulted in success in the past. Deciding the cause of a symptom is often the most difficult step in the breakthrough sequence. And some consider it a breakthrough in knowledge. It demands a deeper knowledge and calls for a statistical and/or a technical analysis for identification.

A statistical analysis relies heavily on quality tools like scatter diagram and product matrix to locate whether the cause relates to any machine, particular operating hour, or operator specific. The technical analysis probes whether the process, material, machine, man or any combination of these influence the variation. A systematic analysis is undertaken to identify the cause: wrong material specification or supply, improper machine setting, inappropriate tools or incorrect way of operation including defects in design and process capability.

It may also involve dealing with management controllable defects, a technical failure analysis is applied to ascertain whether the instructions issued to operators are such that there is scope for different persons to interpret differently. Detailed probable causes on the basis of Ishikawa's Fishbone diagram (also called cause-and-effect analysis) would present all possibilities to be considered by the operators, supervisors and experts with sufficient knowledge and understanding of the process to underpin the root cause.

7.12.4 Remedial Action: When the causes are identified, the remedy must follow so that there are no resulting defects in product. The measures required to be taken are more far reaching and long-term in order to achieve a breakthrough-remedy that would substantially reduce the defects and the company gains from improvement. The remedy may involve change in design, modification of manufacturing process or training of the operator for improving performance.

At times, there appears a risk for sub-optimization. The

implementing team and quality committee with the support of management should work towards optimization within the company and minimization of customer costs for the product to get a clear marketing advantage *vis-à-vis* the competitors.

Action as decided should be taken for effecting change with proper planning for implementation. It is necessary to measure the effects of change and that is the proof of the need. The improving process must be properly planned and continuous. It is effected in 4 different phases, represented by Deming's PDCA cycle:

1. **P** for Plan, which means plan before acting.
2. **D** for Do, perform what has been planned.
3. **C** for Check, verify the results.
4. **A** for Act, standardize if the results are positive, repeat the process and if negative, requires proper analysis for suitable solution set.

Each process of improvement implies a prior precise definition of a project, i.e. a problem whose solution has been planned. Achieving improvements inspires all concerned: management is happy with expected gains, operators are motivated that their product finds better acceptability and customer satisfaction.

7.12.5 Evaluation: Collection of feedback information and analysis is essential to know that the process has improved. It is a great motivating factor for implementing projects subsequently. Fundamental requirements for reaching concrete results are: one, the convinced involvement of people at all levels (workers, supervisors, managers including directors and people of all departments) including participation of different groups in synergy towards common goals, and two, the knowledge for detection and development of appropriate strategy. And in order to achieve the desired result, systematic organization for improvement is essential.

7.13 Launching a New Product

A manufacturing unit is engaged primarily to process

inputs for producing desired output. This is the way millions of units are producing billions of products world over with huge investments in man, machine, capital and technology contributing to the economic progress. Each unit strives to sustain and grow. And in the present era where 'survival of the fittest' rules, a company capable of occasionally launching a new product in order to meet the market demand succeeds. It is one of the ways of expansion and requires a great deal of effort: development from idea to manufacture and offer the product in the market. The product (output) however invariably passes through a definite sequence of phases: (a) definition phase, (b) the preliminary design phase, (c) final design phase, (d) preproduction phase, (e) production phase, and (f) use phase.

A brief description of important functions related to each phase is presented along with highlighting the department logically assigned to take prime and collateral responsibility.

7.13.1 The Definition Phase: The information from any source collected by the marketing research department including ideas and suggestions received are analyzed and translated into a manufacturable product. Similar products available in the market are also studied to compare and ascertain that there exists a gap (demand) for the new entrant. Care is also taken to include certain novel design features that the existing products do not offer. The quality department sets the quality and safety requirements including conformance to environmental conditions.

Prime responsibility : Product Development
Collateral responsibility : Market Research/Quality

7.13.2 Preliminary Design Phase: The drawing and design work begins and first prototype is made and tested. The report of the quality tests are analysed and deficiencies noted are complied with.

Prime responsibility : Design Department
Collateral responsibility : Quality Department

7.13.3 Final Design Phase: In this phase, the design of the product is finalized. Tests including type testing, reliability testing are carried out and deficiencies found are rectified by re-design as required.

Prime responsibility : Design Department
Collateral responsibility : Production Department

7.13.4 Preproduction Phase: This is a very important phase prior to full scale production and requires coordination of the design department, production department and quality department, i.e. the different functions and activities within the company which will affect the quality of product. The following are finalized in this phase:

1. The drawings with clear specifications are prepared for operators and quality department.
2. Different alternatives available for manufacture or outsourcing are evaluated and the optimal choice is decided.
3. Procurement action starts with vendor selection, schedule of requirement.
4. Machines and tools required for the manufacture are selected based on the process capability analysis to meet the quality demands.
5. Training of operators, as required, are provided for.
6. The quality department also finalizes the inspection plan, identifies the process variables that must be specially controlled during the manufacturing process to get quality output along with control charts for production process.

Prime responsibility : Production Department
Collateral responsibility : Quality Department and Marketing department

7.13.5 Production Phase: The full scale production begins with quality inspection as planned so that the product conforms to specification.

Prime responsibility : Production Department
Collateral responsibility : Quality Department/Design Department

7.13.6 Use Phase: It is very important phase for the launch of new product. When the product reaches the market for the first time, the consumer acceptance and their satisfaction are critical to the success. It is the proof of all that has been put into. The feedback information received and collected from the consumer is useful to the management for evaluation and improvement in quality as required.

Prime responsibility : Marketing Department
Collateral responsibility : Quality Department

End Notes

1. Quality plays a key role in keeping costs low, revenue high and profit robust (Johnson, 1991:9).
2. Internal partnering is creating an environment and establishing mechanism within it that brings managers, employees, teams and every individual in the organization together in mutually supportive alliances for better relationships that ultimately would reflect in the output.
3. An organization may have teams like lead team, functional team, cross-functional team and task team for project/process requirement.
4. Crosby, Philip B. 'Completeness: Quality for the 21st Century' Dutton, New York, 1992: xi.
5. To Juran, 'Improvement happens project by project and in no other way' and he defines a project as 'a problem scheduled for solution.
6. Anthony, Maddox and Wheatley in *'Envisionary Management'* conclude that 'the enterprise vision is the integrative synthesis, the conceptual crystallization of the future desired results that both legitimizes and energizes stakeholders'.
7. Richards, M. D. in *'Setting Strategic Goals and Objectives'* clarifies the difference between goal and objective (1987:12).
8. There are a number of approaches; the analytic approach relies on a conscious, top-down, linear flow-chart model, the intuitive approach emphasizes more on imaginative bottom-up model, the political approach decides as per the power of influence, the customer value approach focuses on the customer driven model based on market research and feedback and the drift approach that lead to strategy utilization on individual/collective factors.
9. Mintzberg in *'The Rise and Fall of Strategic Planning'* argues

that strategy formation requires 'coupling of analysis and intuition'.

10. Tom Peters in his interview in 2001 desired to add to them, capabilities concerning ideas, liberation, and speed.

8

Conclusions

Efficiency is 'doing things right' and Effectiveness is 'doing right things'.— Drucker

By now we are sufficiently familiar with the fact that quality as an attribute is associated with only positive aspects of anything: an object, a creation, action and so on. And in business parlance, it relates to a product or service and is judged by the consumer with regard to the stated and implied capability to function properly in addition to its safety and reliability in use. We have also discussed that industry has used quality as an instrument successfully for attaining excellence in output with judicious application of appropriate quality tools, techniques, systems, strategies that have been developed over the years. Indeed, the development process has been phenomenal and there is scholarly unanimity that very few disciplines have seen as many changes as the practice of managing quality in industry. The approaches still continue to evolve; being refined and enriched by research, practical experience and innovative application.

In the present era of globalization, the producers' concern about quality is imperative because it is the key parameter that uniquely integrates the organizational effort and enables the systems and processes for quality output with improved productivity and efficiency. It has also been proved beyond doubt that the companies pursuing quality are better equipped not only to face today's challenges but also to cope with the emerging future. And in keeping with Juran's prediction that 'the twentieth century has been the century for productivity, the twenty-first century will be for quality', its importance seems increasing further.

8.1 Development Praxis

The practice of managing quality in industry is based on the philosophy encompassing fundamental principles advocated by Taylor's simplification of work, division of labour to concepts and approaches developed by pioneers like Shewhart, Deming, Juran, Crosby and Ishikawa among others. It began with inspection of manufactured goods by simply separating bad from the lot, evolved through quality and reliability engineering, quality assurance, to companywide quality (total quality) and quality management as a system approach since the second half of twentieth century.

Today, an enterprise has an option to willingly introduce total quality systems (concept, tools and techniques) with a clear objective of focusing primarily upon to drive an overall improvement of the organization in as much as enhancing the calibre of the people associated with it. Experiences too evince that companies achieve improved efficiency and productivity as a result of the implementation of quality programmes because it uniquely embraces 'doing things right' and 'doing right things'. And in the process, all stakeholders gain and:

1. The management is happy with increased profitability.
2. The workers and supervisors are motivated with a sense of satisfaction that they have made a difference.
3. The consumers get quality product at competitive price.
4. An enhanced image of the company as a whole.

The gains achieved are profound; for example, Japan used the basic concepts, innovatively adapted to its socio-economic environment and established new benchmark in performance. The important factors that contributed to its successes include:

1. Adaptation: Japan adapted the technology and management tools borrowed from the West, blending with human aspects for managing change.
2. Motivation: its strong motivation to experiment new ideas and apply universally when proved useful.
3. Learning from failure: Japanese industries consider 'defects a treasure', meaning there by that much can be

learned from real life experiences while searching for a solution to remedy defects.

In fact, Japan took the lead when industry in other industrialized countries, particularly the United States where most of the concepts developed, saddled with resistance to change and failed to apply new approaches in industry. The hallmark features of the learning experience from Japanese industry and trade are their ability:

1. To transform ideas into products in very short time.
2. To take advantage of state-of-the-art technology, modern management techniques.
3. To adapt quickly to new market conditions, prudently blending the borrowed technology with social ethos and environmental necessity.
4. To manufacture products of outstanding quality, that is realizing the objective.

8.2 The Indian Scene

Initiative for implementation of quality measures in industry in India for attaining quality product and services is very recent. Consequent to policy liberalization in early 1990s, the industry and trade in India faced challenges of international competition and soon realized the necessity of introducing quality concepts for improving production processes for survival and growth. It has been a welcome development and the development seems imbued to one or more of the following factors:

8.2.1 Need for Quality Improvement: Post-Independence, India pursued an inward looking policy regime with wide ranging restrictions for industry, trade and business, placing high emphasis on self-reliance ignoring other aspects like comparative advantage, productivity gains through technology, competition and above all quality. A high internal demand and supply limitations resulted in complacency in industry circles because they could sell whatever they produced. By early 1990s, the country witnessed unprecedented changes in industry and trade policy with economic liberalization. Consequently the industry has since been subjected to competition from within and outside and it industry realizes the need for improving quality and customer orientation.

8.2.2 Awareness of the Gains Achievable: The economic turnaround in Japan and other East Asian countries became visible and that story about their success spread. The management started to realize that quality improvement can often be associated with lower cost of product for achieving competitiveness. Many companies initiated quality measures forming quality circles, obtaining ISO certification for trade expansion. On the whole, the management visualizes possibility for the following:

- **Increasing Profit in the Company:** Information received through the literature on quality, quality consultants validate that improvement in quality is associated with reduction in waste and scrap, better performance efficiency and increase in productivity. Better quality product at reduced cost certainly increases sales and thereby increasing profitability. [1]
- **Improving the Brand Image:** There is no denying the fact that a brand image is fully dependent on the quality of the product. It too has profound effect on the sales of the company's product.
- **Better Employees Motivation:** the employees feel proud to be associated with an improved image of the company, for it is the result of their hard work. The workforce is motivated for better performance and consequently achievement of overall gain of the enterprise.

8.2.3 Enlightened Customers: Customers could be broadly divided into two groups, industrial buyers and general consumers. While industry invariably places its demand of requirements with detailed technical specification and have elaborate vendor evaluation procedure, the individual consumers generally go by market opinion. A majority of them are also not sufficiently educated what to ask for and tend to rely on the advertisement and promises. Of late, the situation in India is changing with increased availability of products from national and international vendors. The customers are in a better position to exercise a choice. They are more enlightened and buy products that meet their needs and preferences. As customers are becoming more sophisticated, better informed and selective, the pressure on the manufacturers for improving the quality of their product is increasing and the only way a business can survive and prosper is by its commitment to quality.

8.3 Whither Quality

The practices that have proved successful are well documented and firms interested to implement quality improvement programmes can take advantage of the development. In fact, it is an ideal option for industry to emulate from the rich experience and chart a proven path for reaching new horizons.

While success are many and failures few, yet it is worth examining the causes for futurity in the true spirit of the total quality approach. Analysis of some instances of unsatisfactory outcome reveals that these companies have generally failed to pay attention, lacked planning and that they bypassed the groundwork necessary for making intelligent choices especially in selection of an implementing agency, deciding priority project for implementation, applying quality approaches and developing systems. As attaining and maintaining quality is an in-company activity, the role of management is crucial to carry forward the organization. And the process should begin with the right step:

1. First, the top management accepts in principle the need for improvement, based on the facts derived from SWOT analysis and Benchmarking Technique,
2. Then, the senior management understands the product, process involved and the areas that need attention. In other

words, they need to understand the goal, the quality processes available to accomplish the goal and the complexity of the processes.

3. And finally, the management decides on the motivation-what the company expects to achieve and the time frame. It evaluates the resource requirement—man, machine, capital, technology and also the limitations. An essential pre-requisite, as discussed earlier, is the supporting infrastructure that would help to reduce and eventually eliminate non-conformance to specifications and standards (wastage) and meet customer expectations in the most cost effective and efficient manner. The management responsibility thus would include:

- Provisioning for resources for the implementation of project.
- Strategizing for success.
- Removing inherent obstacles-employing FTA.
- Establishing an evaluation system for monitoring progress and providing information to all.

8.4 Management Option

Theoretically, all quality processes are roughly grouped into three levels by degree of possible benefit and severity of required change. The amount of change that can be expected being proportional to the motivation driving it, the company needs to evaluate the quality performance in its present stage, the mode of conducting business, its resources, market position including the vision of the management. Then the managers responsible for quality management must understand the efforts required to realize the vision and accordingly choose from the available levels of quality improvement options, i.e. the degree of change required to be effective from amongst the three levels:

1. **Improvement:** Improvement is limited to rectification of problem in the existing processes. Quality improvement at this level deals with routine problems, utilizing the

knowledge and expertise available within the organization.

2. **Redesign:** It involves change and modification of existing design to eliminate inherent problems. It entails application of new quality approaches for success.
3. **Reengineering:** It is a quantum change in situation. Requires visionary leadership to guide a complete change in the way things are being done to the way it should be. It employs new technology, sophisticated equipments and modern methods.

Quality improvement within level one (sporadic problems as discussed in chapter 6) is well within the comfort zone of established practice and is therefore easier than level two or three. The improvement within level two (refers to application of Deming's principles) and level three requires changes that may go beyond the boundaries of all that managers have learned about managing. The managers are not in a position to realize this when they buy into a quality-improvement process and are, therefore, not prepared to deal with it. Would they tackle quality improvement at these levels if they understood the risk? Certainly, those who are sufficiently motivated to attempt radical change are better prepared to make decision and because of it, they would have a much better chance at success.

8.5 Planning for Success

The traditional view that quality problems are either generally of a technical nature to be solved by the technically qualified personnel at the workstation, or in the respective departments and in few cases due to lack of motivation to be taken care of by administrative action have since changed. The management has started appreciating that in most cases, the existing processes and systems have been strained to the limits of their performance resulting in disappointing results and that the goals set could be achieved through total quality, continuous improvement of quality coupled with managerial re-engineering.

The management thus should direct its action in coeval with the organization's philosophy for realization of the set objective. Its responsibilities are not only to initiate, strategize and support improvement but also to set aside time and resources for quality activities and most importantly, introducing change in corporate philosophy, from typical business performance, return on investment and stock price to creating best value for customers and motivating all employees for active participation in the movement to achieve common goal-meeting and exceeding customers' needs.

The implementation should begin with eliciting co-operation of all employees through their empowerment, that is creating knowledge with planned education and training and more importantly establishing a system of open communication—presenting information about the quality situation of the company and how the proposed action plan would benefit not only the shareholder (increasing return on investment) but also the employees at all levels including the customers. As the organization aims at complete transformation, the information that would be of interest to employees may include the following:

1. The action plan, explaining the purpose and assigning clearly the responsibility of departments concerned with quality should be published as an official document.
2. A definite quantitative target by way of sales or revenue to be generated in a reasonable time frame along with resource allocation for achieving the target.
3. Periodic review of reports based on a system of measurement for monitoring quality of product and process prepared highlighting points with regard to the progress of implementation, improvement and tangible gains by the management and for information to all employees.

International standard ISO 9001 provides for a management framework—a quality management system (QMS) necessary to control and address risks, measure and monitor business performance, apply techniques for continuous improvement scientifically and there by enhance company's image. The standard ISO 9001 series though originally developed for products, especially manufactured products, its scope has since widened to include to any business or non-business activity: design work, administrative services, consulting, banking, insurance, computer software development, retailing, transportation, education and so on. A 'product' in ISO vocabulary presently means a physical object, services, including software.

8.6 Quality in Services

The quality improvement process being generic in the sense that it can be applied to any activity, the influence of quality thinking has spread to non-traditional applications outside of walls of manufacturing, extending into service sectors and into areas such as sales, marketing and customer service. The nature of activities seems to be changing: the manufacturing companies prefer to outsource a part of their work, especially specialized knowledge based tasks. The production function is becoming dependent on services. There is thus need for quality improvement in the services offered by service providers. There seems a justified case for quality management in every sector of industry.

It is more relevant for today's Indian business environment than ever before. The country in the new millennium has emerged as a major service exporter, experienced substantial growth in exports and created a formidable presence in international market which even America abhors. Opportunities exist and the emergent scenario demands a paradigm shift in approach to sustain and expand. The industry must appreciate the need and initiate action in the right direction.

8.7 Prospects for Quality

Some experts believe that the ideas promoted by the men of vision in the domain of quality management (Taylor to

Shewhart, Juran to Ishikawa) were appropriate in their time and helped realize great advances in productivity, but they are perhaps inadequate to deal with the problems in the present scenario. Though today's modern business enterprises operate under the same fundamental principle, like the division and simplification of work, it tends to utilize workers with higher skills, more and more specialization. The development due to breaking up the value chain and outsourcing have created certain constraints which include one, labour-management relations; two, defining organizational policy and communicating with employees; and three, managing the downsizing realities.

All these aspects strictly, do not relate to quality, but to the work of human relations. The barriers can be overcome by addressing the issues involved focusing on systems of the organization. Ackoff (1993) notes that 'the focus of total quality movement should be on work that's fun, and workers enjoying a higher quality of work life. Then the quality of products and services will take care of itself.' He also advocates that the orientation needs to be based on the following:

1. Focus on removing defects of systems/sub-systems (process) for improvement in quality alone is inadequate.
2. A company has to aim at breakthrough improvement rather than incremental approach to improvement for competing in today's dynamic market conditions.
3. A need obviously exists to transform the structure and culture of the organizations so that they are better equipped to meet the challenges of time.
4. Quality should be defined as meeting or exceeding the expectations of all stakeholders, not the customer alone as is being practiced.

Deming succinctly presents his idea, 'Improvement is not a one-time effort. The management is obliged to continually look for ways to reduce waste and improve quality.' It is because customer needs and preferences are continuously changing, because the technology for is fast changing, because new processes for design and manufacture are continuously being innovated. Developments being continuous, improvement must be an ongoing process for any industry to achieve success.

In any event, managing total quality ought to form a habit of the management team. It is proved to be an easy path to success. The research findings of George and Weimerskirch (2003) brilliantly confirm the stimulating experience of companies pursuing total quality, 'In our experience, the companies that involve everyone in continuous improvement, that make customer satisfaction their top priority, that value people for who they are and that their systems as treasure chests filled with endless opportunities-these companies have the most joyful, outgoing and well-rewarded people we know...They stand on the riverbank called TQM and shout out the wonders of working together for good of all.' Their enthusiasm is infectious, their commitment inspiring.

It is also believed that the development beyond total quality in the 21st century will have profound implications for a company pursuing quality objectives. Total systems integration is considered to be crucial for success of total quality and beyond. Environmental conditions are considered as key concerns by many and leadership has to deftly manage change. The total quality objective must ensure a clear and well defined vision: to outperform the past and competitors for meeting and exceeding customer delight. And the management capable of providing leadership for continuous improvement, imbibing the spirit of unifying individual and organizational goal in the employees would certainly succeed in their endeavour to establish a total quality organization and quality culture. This perhaps is the essence of **'Quality Management in Industry'**.

End Note

1. Research analysis reveals that quality improvement increases return on investment in all sectors of industry.

Appendix

Appendix

Quality Improvement in a Service Organization: A Case Study of Saraswati Vidyapeeth, Balasore

---

Background:

Balasore (Odisha) is a fast growing town in the Eastern coast. A substantial portion of its population could be placed in the middle class by local income standards and most of them in this social segment have developed a fancy to educate their wards in an English medium school. And in keeping with the emerging trend, a few such schools have been set up in the town to meet the demand.

Inspired by the development, a group of professionals have decided to promote an English medium senior secondary school to cater to a niche demand that exists in the town and its vicinity. The project has been implemented and a school is functioning for the last six years. The school made a humble beginning in 2005 with a few students in nursery class in rented premises in the town and every year one or two classes have been added. Gradually, the classes and the student strength increased. By 2010, it has created its own infrastructure—the school building and other facilities at a distance of 5 km. from the town, in a rural setting where it has started functioning from the pre-nursery to standard VI with effect from April 1, 2011.

At this stage (June 2011) a consultant is engaged to intervene for efficient management of the institution and the implementation of the improvement programme follows.

Evaluation of Existing Status

The first step towards initiating a project and designing strategy for improvement is assessment of the existing systems and processes, discuss with the management for moving forward.

The important components of the organization that directly or indirectly contribute to the overall growth comprise the location, the management philosophy, the teachers, the students and the parents.

Location: The school is situated at a place about 5 km. away from the town. The distance though is not too far, for the students residing at Balasore, it is a long journey: the road condition forces even a straight drive half an hour and for the school vehicle to pick up students from the lanes and by lanes, it is almost one hour.

The parents, only on this score, show reluctance to admit their children here especially in pre-primary and primary classes. And as a result, they take admission in other schools and continue there. The location thus does not contribute positively to the growth of the school.

Management: The promoters comprise 18 individuals mostly qualified working professionals or businessmen. They however do not participate in managing the affairs of the school except exchange of e-mails for information or suggestion. The secretary of the promoting society takes active interest and keen to be in-charge of each and every activity of the institution. He is a professional but pursues a traditional style for managing functions of the school, perhaps influenced by his past experience and/or limitations. He nourishes a strong feeling that the school is one of the best—a reflection of the 'internal quality', as discussed in the book, unaware of 'true quality' that is far from satisfactory due to plethora of problems and weaknesses that prevail.

Teachers: With the exception to one or two, all teachers are young graduate/post-graduates. Some of them have limited teaching experience, either in a small school or home tuition. Most of them are enthusiastic to learn, but lack of opportunity to get guidance and their weak background especially communicating in English has impeded development since

English is crucial for imparting proper education in an English medium school.

In addition, there exist sub-cultures that militate against team spirit essential for establishing a quality organization. This may have developed due to the influence of local tradition or by seer habit of some.

Students: At present there seems no strong motivation for the parents to consider this school as an ideal option for their words to pursue schooling here. The location of the school and its inherent limitations like two hours journey a day and no name tag yet fail to convince the aspiring parents that the school is in a position to offer better education than similar other schools. In the circumstances, only those who could not secure admission or continue due to some reason in a comparable good school decide to get admitted here. Besides, the school in its eagerness to reach a breakeven point in the circumstances, creating a competitive academic environment with average to weak category of students becomes rather difficult.

Analysis and Discussion

In order to logically conclude the real state, a SWOT analysis for identifying the weak areas that need to be improved and a comparative analysis by benchmarking technique have been attempted.

Strength of the Organization: The obvious positive aspects are the available infrastructure facilities and commitment of the management for providing resources for achieving success.

Weakness: The weaknesses in the system seem to pervade every sphere of activity of the organization, which include the following:

1. The management need to understand and appreciate the problems that must be addressed adequately for desired result.
2. The teachers need training and motivation to change for

imparting 'good education', for it is the prime function of the school.

3. The students need improvement not only in their studies, but more importantly in discipline, which is vital for academic pursuits. Efforts are necessary to attract good student to the school to provide an impetus to the overall learning environment.
4. The other associated systems and sub-systems, e.g. transportation, hostel, time table too need attention as these influence the curriculum: improper time schedule of without considering their capability has been a deterrent to providing quality teaching.

Opportunity: scope exists for growth subject to managing certain key parameters for augmentation.

Threats: There are threats from external as well as internal: while the external factors arise from a large number of schools advertising to offer modern teaching blended with Indian heritage including a very low fee structure, the internal relates to the persons associated with the institution: their action sometimes de-motivates and impedes the improvement process. It adversely affects accomplishing the goal.

Benchmarking: There are a few English medium secondary and senior secondary schools in the town and their existence vary from about a decade to four decades. These schools have taken advantage of the demand at an opportune time and now enjoy the market reputation they have acquired. They in true sense have not developed something model or novel that should be emulated. Their reputation by and large seems mere perception. The parents are generally happy as their children get very good 'report card' which they could boastfully present to the known and the unknown.

They are blissfully unaware of the real calibre of their children. The schools adopt such practice on order to gain popularity that they are offering good education with substantial evidence from the report card. It helps them to gain the patronage of the parents who also encourage other parents to admit their wards.

These schools however have developed a sense of complacency which could be exploited to the school's advantage only by proper action: deft management of the resources for imparting 'quality education'.

Some Important Aspects: The management including teachers though are vociferous that they are one of the best school in the town in so far as developing students, the curriculum they pursue seems to have been missing the basics:

1. As much as the school in its six years of existence never considered hand writing practice an essential part of teaching a language especially in the pre-primary level.
2. The teachers do not care to communicate in English, despite complaints by parents.
3. The students lack basic discipline in conducting themselves even in the class rooms and a usual rationalization given by teachers that 'we cannot punish them'.
4. The situation, as it is at present, has developed over the past five years and is mostly management related. In the circumstances, initiating a programme for improving quality appeared a daunting challenge, for it necessitated change of almost all systems and processes.

Management Response

A discussion with the management is essential prior to implementation because the project for improvement would depend to a great extent on the vision of the management, their commitment to provide resources and most importantly their motivation with regard to the level of improvement desired, as discussed in chapter 8.

The management readily appreciated the need for improvement and extended their commitment and resources required for the project to accomplish the goal.

And keeping in view that: (a) the core activity of the organization relates to offering 'quality education', and (b) the service offered must conform to the stated or implied specification, i.e. 'fitness for use' to meet and exceed customers expectation, the strategies developed for implementation are discussed.

Step 1: Focusing on the Primary Activity

The first step is always decisive for the programme. It signals change and as usual, enlists co-operation of some and prepares to face resistance from others during implementation. Experience suggests that a judicious and pragmatic strategy should help to move forward. The support of the people who are responsible in some way in contributing to quality being crucial, they have to be motivated with information about the programme and the expected result.

Against this backdrop, the project commenced with a clear objective, to focus on 'open communication' with those who contribute to quality in order to elicit their involvement for improvement. The present status and the goal to be achieved were therefore candidly discussed with the management and teachers and suggestions invited for finalizing strategy.

Teachers' Response: All agreed in principle that the change is necessary for imparting proper instruction. It was discussed and unanimously decided that method of instruction should change: that students from standard III onwards must understand and write, as against the normal practice that teachers write down the answers which the students copy and memorise by rote.

In a few days it was clear that some teachers could not perceive what is really expected of them where as some hesitated to change as they felt 'what is wrong with what we have been doing so far?' The process so far being followed has satisfied all: it was easy for the teachers to write the answers which the students easily remembered, wrote the same in the test, scored good marks and the parents were happy to note that their children were bright. Hardly anyone cared to realize that it benefited none: the students could not gain the required knowledge—developing the capacity to read, write, understand and speak, the teachers in the circumstances wasted their time and energy as they have not succeeded to impart education, as desired.

As a strategy for managing change, the programme was introduced with those willing to accept new initiative.

Parents' Response: The parents are the customers and it was considered prudent to inform them in the Parents Teachers Meeting. The co-operation of the parents was elicited since the development of the child is essentially a joint responsibility of the parents and teachers. The new initiative for imparting quality education was clearly explained along with the principle behind such a move-what is being planned and why.

And a surprise reaction from an unexpected quarter—most of the parents showed high resistance and a few who did not openly oppose, did not support, either. This could be their limitation or indifference. During the next meeting that was after a period of two months parents by and large complained that their children have become weak in studies. It became evident that their only way of assessing the development of a child was marks in the regular weekly test.

They could neither understand nor appreciate that the marks their words used to obtain earlier did not really reflect their knowledge; that they, even after years of regular schooling are unable to write a few sentences correctly and that the new method is an attempt to rectify the system for the betterment of the students. Considering that it could partly be due to resistance to change and partly their perception about good education, the objective was explained again in greater detail. And to our dismay, it also came to the notice that some of the teachers who opposed change in the routine or method of instruction interacted with the parents and even tacitly requested for such a reaction.

Step 2: Associated Systems and Sub-systems

Simultaneously the other systems and sub-systems that

influenced improvement of quality of education were considered for augmentation. The two main areas associated with the project were: (a) transportation, and (b) allotment of subjects to teachers.

The transportation affected the study because some students who arrived too late missed classes. In addition the delayed departure of kids beyond the school time made them too hungry and restless.

And prior to allocating the subjects to the teachers, they were asked to confirm their competence with regard to the subject depending upon their academic background and teaching experience. The time-table was finalized with concensus.

Step 3: Induction of Better Students

Improvement of quality of student has been a great concern. Induction of some good students was considered imperative in order to create a sense of competition amongst the students and good environment for study in the school. Towards achieving this end, a mental and scholastic aptitude test was organised for students of standard V and VI offering scholarship for the top five up to standard X. Students of class V and VI from all schools were invited to participate.

A few good students presently reading in other English medium schools participated in the test, scored good marks but as usual, most of them are not inclined to join this school leaving their school which has a 'name tag' and classes up to senior secondary level. The efforts however continue to motivate some.

Conclusion

The inherent problems notwithstanding, by January, 2012 the effect of change seems to have gradually influenced most: the management though were sceptical in the beginning, seems now more confident that the programme would certainly show positive effect, the teachers are more amenable to change and at least some parents have expressed their satisfaction.

It is however important to note the basic tenets that:

1. Managing change has never been easy. The present instance too confirms.
2. The project has to be introduced keeping in view the critical processes and systems and with due regard to the socio-cultural environment of all stakeholders, especially the key players.
3. And another important point the managers and consultants must keep in mind while introducing an improvement programme is that development is a long-term process. In fact, tangible results are not instantaneous. Accomplishing desired goal may take some time.

References

References

Ackoff, Russell L. '*Beyond Total Quality Management*' The Journal for Quality and participation, March 1993.

Almeida, E., Alvaro, A., Meria, S. '*Quality Assurance process*' Foundation of Software Engineering, September3, 2007.

Akao, Y. '*Quality Function Deployment: Integrating Customer Requirement into product Design*' Productivity Press, Portland, 1990.

Akao, Yoji '*Development History of Quality Function Deployment - The Customer Driven Approach to Quality Planning and Deployment*' Asian Productivity Organization, Japan, 1994.

Almeida, E., A. Alvaro and S. Meria '*A Component Quality Assurance Process*' Foundations of Software Engineering, September 3-4, 2007.

Anderson Consulting '*The Second lean Enterprise Report*' Anderson Consulting, London, 1994

Binney, G. '*Making Quality Work: Lessons from Europe*' Economic Intelligence, London, 1992.

Bossert, James, L. '*Quality Function Deployment: A Practitioner's Approach*' ASQC Quality Press, 1991.

Bothe, D. R. '*Measuring Process Capabilities*' McGraw Hill, New York, 1997.

Bross, Irwin '*Design for Decision*' Macmillan Publishing Company, 1953.

Cameron, Kim '*An Empirical Investigation of Quality Culture, Practice and Outcomes*' Paper presented at the Annual Meetings of the Academy of Management, Dallas, 1994.

Chowdhury, S. '*Design for Six Sigma*' Kaplan Professional Company, Chicago, 2002.

Cole, R. '*Introduction*, Special Issue-*Total Quality Management*' California Management Review, 35(3), 1993.

Covey, Stephen R. '*Principle Cantered Leadership*' Summit Books, New York, 1991.

Crosby, P. B. '*Quality is Free: The Art of making Quality Certain*' Mentor, New York, 1979.

Crosby, Philip B. '*Completeness: Quality for the 21st Century*' Plume, 1994.

Dale, B. '*Managing Quality*' Prentice Hall, 1994.

Dale, B. and C. Cooper '*Total Quality and Human Resource: An Executive Guide*' Blackwell, 1992.

Das, Kamal '*Managing Development*', Global Research Publication, 2010.

Davenport, Thomas H '*Process Innovation*' Harvard Business Press, 1992.

Dawson, P. '*Organizational Change: A Procedural Approach*' Chapman, London, 1994.

Dawson, P. and G. Palmer (ed.) '*Total Quality Management: Breaking the Myth*' Longman Cheshire, 1994.

De Bono, Edward '*Six Thinking Hats: An Essential Approach to Business Management*' Little, Brown and Company, 1985.

Deal, T. and A. Kennedy '*Corporate Culture*' Addison-Wesley, 1992.

Dean, J. and D. Bowen '*Management Theory and Total Quality: improving research and practice through theory development*' Academy of management review, 19(3), 1994.

DeFeo, Joseph A. "*The Future Impact of Quality*" Quality Engineering, Volume 13, Number 3, 2001.

Deming, W. E. '*Out of Crisis*' Cambridge University Press, 1986.

Deming, W. E. '*Quality, Productivity and Competitive Position*' MIT Centre of Advanced Engineering Study, 1982.

Dodge, H. F. and H. G. Roming '*Sampling Inspection Tables; Single and Double Sample*' Wiley, New York, 1959.

Drummond, H. '*The Quality Movement: What Total Quality Management is all about*' Kogan Page, London, 1992.

Dumas, Ronald A. Quality Progress, 1989.

Easton, George S. '*Total Quality Management: A Baldrige Examiner's Perspective*' California Management Review, Spring, 1993.

Evans, J. and W. Lindsay '*The Management and Control of Quality*' West Publishing, 1993.

Feigenbaum, A. V. '*Total Quality Control*' McGraw Hill, 1983.

Fletcher, C. '*Appraisal: Routes to Improved Performance*' Institute of Personnel Management, London, 1993.

Flood R. L. '*Beyond Total Quality Management*' John Wiley and Sons, 1992.

Fredrikson B. '*Holistic system engineering in Product Development*' The Saab-Scania Griffin, Sweden, November, 1994.

Fukuda, Ryuji 'CEDAC: A Tool for Continuous Systemic

Improvement' Productivity Press, Cambridge, 1989.

Gabor, A. '*The Man Who Invented Quality*' Penguin, 1990.

Garvin, D. '*Managing Quality*' Free Press, New York, 1988.

Garvin, David A. '*What does Product Quality really mean?*' Sloan Management Review, Vol. 26, No. 1, 1984.

George, M. L. '*Lean Six Sigma for Service: How to Use Lean Speed and Six sigma to Improve Services and Transactions*' McGraw Hill, New York, 2003.

Geotsch, David L., Stanley Davis '*Introduction to Total Quality*' Macmillan, 1994.

Godfrey, A. B. '*Juran's Quality Handbook*' S. Feldman, 2005.

Goldratt, Avraham Y. '*Theory of Constraints*' The Goldratt Institute, Undated Paper.

Hackman, R. and R. Wageman '*Total Quality Management: empirical, conceptual and practical issues*' Administrative Science Quarterly, 40, June 1995.

Hammer, M. and J. Champy '*Re-engineering the Corporation: A Manifesto for a Business Revolution*' Harper Business, New York, 1994.

Harry, M. J. '*Six Sigma: A Breakthrough Strategy for Profitability*' Quality Progress, May 1998.

Harry, M. J. '*The Vision of Six Sigma: A Roadmap for Breakthrough*' Sigma Publishing Company, Phoenix, 1994.

Hill, S. '*From Quality Circle to Total Quality Management*' in Wilkinson, A and H. Willmott (ed.) Making Quality Circle, Routledge, London, 1995.

Hill, S. and A. Wilkinson '*In Search of Total Quality Management*' Employees Relations 17(3), 1995.

Hockman, Kimberly K. '*Taking Mystery out of Quality*' Training and Development, July 1992.

Hutchins, David C. '*Hoshin Kanri: the strategic approach to continuous improvement*' Gower Publishing, 2008.

Hutchins, David C. '*Just In Time*' Gower Publishing, 1999.

Hutchins, David C. '*The Quality Circles Handbook.*' Pitman Press, New York, 1985.

Hutchins, David C. '*Hoshin Kanri: the strategic approach to continuous improvement*' Gower, Vermount, September, 2008.

Hyde, A. C. '*Barriers in Implementing Quality Management*' The Public Manager-The New Bureaucrat, Spring, 1993.

Imai, Masaaki 'Kaizen: The Key to Japan's Competitive Success'

McGraw Hill, New York, 1986.

Imai, Masaaki '*Kaizen: The Key to Japan's Competitive Success*' Random House, New York, 1986.

Ishikawa, K and D. Lu '*What is Total Quality Control? The Japanese Way*' Prentice-Hall, 1985.

Ishikawa, Kaoru '*What is Total Quality Control? The Japanese Way*' Prentice Hall, 1985.

Ishikawa, Kaoru '*What Is Total Quality Control? The Japanese Way*' Prentice Hall, 1985.

Jacob, Rahul '*TQM: More than a Dying Fad*' Fortune, October 18, 1993.

Johansson, Henry J., Patrick McHugh, A. Pendleburg, A. John and William Wheeler III 'Business Process Reengineering' John Wiley and Sons, 1993.

Johnson, Perry L. *Total Quality Management*' Perry Johnson Inc. 1991.

Johnson, Richard S. '*TQM: Leadership for Quality Transformation*' ASQC Quality Press, 1993.

Juran, J. M. '*Managerial Breakthrough*' McGraw Hill, 1964.

Juran, J. M. '*Quality Control Handbook*' McGraw Hill, 1974.

Juran, J. M. '*The Quality Trilogy: a universal approach to managing quality*' Quality Progress, August, 1986.

Juran, Joseph M '*The Quality Trilogy*' Quality Progress, August, 1986.

Juran, Joseph M. '*Why Quality Initiatives Fail*' Journal of Business Strategy, Vol.14, No.4, Jul/Aug, 1993: 35-38.

Juran, Joseph M. '*Juran on Leadership for Quality*' The Free press, New York, 1989.

Juran, Joseph M. '*Juran on quality by design: the new steps for planning quality into goods and services*' Free Press, New York, 1992.

Kochan, Thomas and Michael Useem (ed.) '*Transforming Organizations*' Oxford University Press, New York, 1994.

Kolesar, P. '*Partial Quality management*' Production and Operations Management, 4(3), 1995.

Kordupleski, R. E., R. T. Rust, and A. J. Zarhorik '*Why Improving Quality does not Improve Quality*' California Management Review, 1993.

Lawler, E. E. III '*High-involvement Management*' Jossey-Bass, 1986.

Lawler, Edward E. '*TQM and Employee Involvement: Are They Compatible?*' The Academy of Management Executive, Vol. 8, No. 1, 1994.

Liker, J. K. '*The Toyota Way*' McGraw Hill, New York, 2004.

Lillrank, P. and N. Kano '*Continuous Improvement: Quality Circle in Japanese Industry*' University of Michigan, 1989.

Lindsay, William M. and Joseph A. Petrick '*Total Quality and Organization Development*' St. Lucie Press, 1997.

Lu, David '*Kanban: Just-in-Time at Toyota*' Productivity Press and Japanese Management Association, 1990.

Maduri, Omnamasivaya '*Understanding and Applying QFD in Heavy Industry*' The Journal for Quality and Participation, Vol. 15, No. 1, January/February 1992.

Meisinger, M. and S. Wagner '*Integrating a Model of Analytical Quality Assurance into the V-Model XT*' Foundations of Software Engineering, November 6, 2006.

Merli, Goirgi '*Total Quality Management*' Productivity Press, 1990

Mintzberg, Henry '*The Rise and Fall of Strategic Planning*' Free Press, New York, 1994.

Monden, Y. '*The Toyota Management System: Linking the Seven Key Functional Areas*' Productivity Press, Portland, 1993.

Montana, Patrick J., Bruce H. Charnov '*Management*' Barron's, 2008.

Montgomery, Douglas '*Introduction to Statistical Quality Control*' John Wiley and Sons, 2005.

Nancy R. Tague '*Seven Basic Tools of Quality The Quality Toolbox*': American Society for Quality, 2004.

Oakland, J. S. '*Total Quality Management: The Route to Improving Performance*' Butterworth-Heinemann, 1993.

Ott, E. R. '*Process Quality Control*' McGraw Hill, 1975.

Pande, P. S., R. P. Newman and R. R. Cavanagh '*The Six Sigma Way: How GE, Motorolla and Other Top companies are Honing their performance*' McGraw Hill, New York, 2000.

Parasuraman, A. V. Zeithaml and L. Berry '*SERVQUAL: A multiple item scale for measuring consumer perceptions of Service Quality*' Journal of Retailing, Vol. 64, No.1, 1988.

Pascale, R. and A. Athos '*The Art of Japanese management*' Allan Lane, 1982.

Peters, T. and R. Waterman '*In Search of Excellence*' Harper and Row, New York, 1982.

Piore, M. J. and C. Sable *'The Second Industrial Divide'* Basic Books, New York, 1984.

Poirier, Charles C. and William F. Hauser *'Business Partnering for Continuous Improvement'* Berrett-Koehler Publishers, 1993.

Powell, T. C. *'Total Quality Management as Competitive Advantage: an empirical study'* Strategic Management Journal, 16(1), 1995.

Pyzdek, T. *'Quality Engineering Handbook'* 2003.

Rampey, J. And H. Roberts *'Perspectives in Total Quality'* Proceedings of Total Quality Forum IV, Cincinnati, November, 1992.

Reger, Rhonda K., Loren T. Gustofson, Samuel M. Demaire and John V. Mullane *'Reframing the Organization: Why Implementing Total Quality is Easier Said than Done'* Academy of Management Review, Vol. 19, No. 3, 1994.

Richards, M. D. *'Setting Strategic Goals and Objectives'* West Publishing, 1987.

Ruskin, John *'Pre-Raphaelitism'* 1851.

Sagan, Carl *'Broca's Brain'* Random House, 1979.

Sandholm, L. *'Japanese Quality Circle'* Quality Progress, February, 1986.

Sandholm, Lennart *'Japanese Quality Circle-a remedy for the West's Quality Problems?'* Quality Progress, February, 1983.

Scholtes, Peter R. *'The Team Handbook'* Joiner Associates Inc. Madison, 1992.

Shewhart, W. A. *'The Applications of Statistics as an Aid in Maintaining Quality in Manufactured Products'* Journal of the American Statistical Association, 1925.

Steingard, D. S. and D. E. Fitzgibbons *'A Post-modern Deconstruction of TQM'* Journal of Organisational Change Management, 6(5) 1993.

Suh, N. *'Axiomatic Design: Advances and Applications'* Oxford University Press, 2001.

Sullivan, L. P. *'Quality Function Deployment'* Quality Progress, May, 1986.

Thareja, Mannu and Priyavrat Thareja *'The Quality Brilliance through Brilliant People'* Quality World 4 (2), 2007.

Townsend, P. L. and Joan E. Gebhardt *'Quality in Action'* John Wiley and Sons, Inc, 1992.

Tuckman, A. *'Ideology, Quality and TQM'* in Wilkinson, A and H. Willmott (ed.) Making Quality Critical: Studies in

Organizational Change, Routledge, London, 1995.

Tuckman, A. '*The Yellow Brick Road: TQM and the restructuring of organisational culture*' Organisation Studies, 15(5), 1994.

Uselac, Stephen '*Zen Leadership: The Human Side of Total Quality Team Management*' Mohican Publishing Company, 1993.

Voehl, Frank, Peter Jackson and David Ashton '*ISO 9000: An Implementation Guide for Small to Medium-sized Business*' Lucie Press, 1994.

Vroman, H. William and V.P. Luchsinger '*Managing Organizational Quality*' Burr Ridge, 1994.

Walton, Mary '*The Deming Management Method*' The Putnam Publishing Group, 1986.

Watson, Gregory H. 'Strategic Benchmarking' John Wiley and Sons, New York, 1993.

Watson, Thomas J. Jr. '*A Business and its Beliefs-The Ideas that Helped Build IBM*' McGraw-Hill, New York, 2003

Weed, Julie '*Factory Efficiency comes to Hospitals*' The New York Times, July 10, 2010.

Whitely, Richard C. '*The Customer driven Company*' Addison-Wesley, New York, 1991.

Wilkinson, A and H. Willmott '*Total Quality–Asking Critical Questions*' Academy of Management Review, 20(4), 1995.

Wilkinson, A. '*Three Road to Quality: Variation in Total Quality Management*' in J. Storey (ed.) Blackwell Cases in HRM, Blackwell, 1996.

Wilkinson, A., M. Marchington, J. Goodman and P. Ackers '*Total Quality Management and Employees Involvement*' Human Resource Management Journal, 2(4), 1992.

Wilkinson, Adrian, Tom Redman, ed. Snape and Mick Marchington '*Managing with TQM*' Macmillan, 1998.

Witcher, B. '*The Changing Scale of Total Quality Management*' Quality Management Journal, Summer, 1995.

Womack, James, Daniel T. Jones and Daniel Roos '*The Machine that Changed the World*' Harper Collins, New York, 1990.

Wyatt, John 'T*he New Deal: What Companies and Employees owe each other*' Fortune, June 13, 1994.

Yahagi, Seiichiro '*After Product Quality in Japan: Management Quality*' National Productivity Review, Autumn, 1992.

Yang, Kai '*Design Six Sigma for Service*' McGraw Hill, New York, 2005.

Zairi, M., S. Letza and J. Oakland *'Does TQM impact on bottom line results?'* TQM Magazine, 6(1) 1994.

Index

Index